MOUNTAINS OF PRAYER

A Story of God's Spectacular Participation in One Man's Life

Barry A. Pratt MA, MFT

TEACH Services, Inc.
P U B L I S H I N G
www.TEACHServices.com • (800) 367-1844

Copyright © 2022 Barry A. Pratt
Copyright © 2022 TEACH Services, Inc.
ISBN-13: 978-1-4796-1469-1 (Paperback)
ISBN-13: 978-1-4796-1470-7 (ePub)
Library of Congress Control Number: 2022900291

The author assumes full responsibility for the accuracy and interpretation of the Ellen White quotations cited in this book.

Published by

TEACH Services, Inc.
P U B L I S H I N G
www.TEACHServices.com • (800) 367-1844

Table of Contents

Preface

I don't remember, exactly anyway, how I first came in contact with Barry Pratt. If what I do remember is correct, a mutual friend connected us, and it was in the context of me working with Barry on his memoirs, his testimony, his spiritual journey. Apparently, his friend—knowing something of Barry's amazing story, his journey to Jesus, and to the Adventist faith—thought that he needed to have it written up, and that I could help.

The rest is history. I have worked in the past with people, helping them take their manuscripts, at various levels of completeness, coherence, and form in general, and did what I could to help shape them into something publishable. This is exactly what I did with Barry's manuscript, which sits in your hands now as *Mountains of Prayer: A Story of God's Spectacular Participation in One Man's Life*.

What a journey—what a spiritual journey—this was, and I was swept up along in it, having of course to read slowly and carefully as an editor. Though my story was completely different than his, there were elements that I could relate to: a young man lost and clueless coming into the wonderful truths of the Adventist Message.

Again, what an excursion it was. More ups and downs than two hyper kids on a seesaw. I don't want to play the spoiler here, and so am not going to say too much, only that if we didn't, to some degree, already know the ending, that Barry became a man of faith (after all, this book wouldn't have been published otherwise), you might have had doubts about how this would indeed end.

For me, and I hope for the reader, what stood out most was Barry's faith: his absolute trust in God's overwhelming and overriding providence, even in the bad times. Truly, as I was editing, I found myself encouraged by his faith, even in the "little things." That is, I would at times tell myself, "Don't forget what Barry wrote and how he handled by faith what came his way." In short, I was ministered to as I read the book, and I believe that readers will be, also.

It's always amazing how the God who put two trillion galaxies (at last count) into the universe, and sustains them as well, could show interest, not just in this earth, but in each individual here, including Barry Pratt. His story shows the truth of Paul's words to the Athenians: "And He has made from one blood every nation of men to dwell on all the face of the earth, and has determined their preappointed times and the boundaries of their dwellings, so that they should seek the Lord, in the hope that they might grope for Him and find Him, though He is not far from each one of us" (Acts 17:26, 27). It's the last clause of that long sentence that's my immediate focus: that God is, indeed, not far from any of us. And that's a truth that becomes amazingly apparent in Barry's story.

And, if He wasn't far from Barry, He's not from each of us, individually; we just need to open our eyes, as did Barry, in order to see Him.

Clifford Goldstein, August 2021

Acknowledgements

When we begin our walk with Jesus, He sends people into our lives to help along the way; to move us in the right direction when stumbling on the upward path to eternal life. I would like to acknowledge a few. The first is Arnie Oettel, PhD, a Sabbath School teacher extraordinaire, and early mentor. My first pastor was Andrew Dahl, who strongly emphasized the value of the Bible in everyday life. Another mentor, Emilio Knechtle, I only met once, but his many sermons on cassette and CD influenced me for decades and helped me establish an understanding of righteousness by faith and the centrality of Jesus in the Adventist faith. Morris Venden's books helped me learn that a vibrant, daily relationship with Jesus is the foundation of the Christian life.

In the area of prayer I was blessed with several people who taught and demonstrated the absolute necessity of prayer in the life of a Christian. One was Naomi Parson, who was the Prayer Coordinator for the Northern California Conference for twenty years—a saint, if there ever was one. Naomi's sister, Ruthie Jacobson, long-time North American Division Prayer Coordinator, demonstrated how perseverance in prayer would lead to joy, blessings, changed lives, and funds when no budget was available. Prayer ministry took off for me during many years at Soquel Camp Meeting when Jerry and Janet Page were conference leaders in Central California. Their dependence on prayer led a revival in that conference.

My current pastor, David Gardner, is the one who started this project, unbeknownst to me. He secretly contacted his friend and author Clifford Goldstein about helping "a man who had some stories." It turned out to be a huge blessing to have Cliff be my "creative guru" in developing the early manuscript. TEACH Services, Inc.'s supervising editor, Rebecca Silver, was a fantastic and patient "shepherd" as the manuscript turned into a book.

Last, but not least, my family, for putting up with me.

Introduction

We are living at a time when our world seems to be careening out of control, with increasing uncertainty and fading faith. People of all faiths, or no faith at all, are looking for some degree of certainty, for some degree of peace, for security, and for answers that satisfy. Luke 21:25 predicts that there will be "distress of nations, with perplexity" just before Jesus comes. I am told the word *perplexity* implies confusion.

Where are you going, friend, for your answers? Where is your god in the midst of this chaos? Is your god up to the task of taking care of you and your family? Is he involved in the daily events of your life? Does your god have this world under control? Is he sovereign over all things, as the Bible proclaims of the God of Abraham, Isaac, and Jacob? Is God still on the throne of the universe?

My life story, a story of God's amazing work in one man's life, will undoubtedly, unabashedly, answer these questions in the most positive sense. As an old radio program declares, "God is still on the throne and prayer changes things" (*The Southwest Radio Church*, 1933). Yes, without a doubt, He is still on the throne. The world is His footstool (see Isa. 66:1). He is passionately, deeply, lovingly involved in every aspect of this world and even in your very life. Every breath, every beat of your heart, comes from Him. His love and concern for you know no bounds. His love for you and this world is so great that He knowingly, willingly, allowed His Son to come here, to be rejected by His own creation, and despised by those He came to save. Yet Jesus chose to die for the world, nay, for the whole universe.

Can you trust a God like that? Can you allow Him to have His way in your life? How can you not?

In this story, a true story, my story, you will see how concerned, patient, all-knowing, and powerful God can be. My story will show God's character and the way He can intervene in a person's life. I have found what God revealed to Moses to be true. Moses asked to see who God was. What He was really like? God graciously revealed what Moses could withstand of His presence and opened his mind to understand.

9

"And the LORD descended in the cloud, and stood with him there, and proclaimed the name of the LORD. And the LORD passed by before him, and proclaimed, The LORD, The LORD God, *merciful* and *gracious, longsuffering*, and abundant in *goodness* and *truth*, keeping mercy for thousands, *forgiving* iniquity and transgression and sin, and that will by *no means clear the guilty*; visiting the iniquity of the fathers upon the children, and upon the children's children, unto the third and to the fourth generation" (Exod. 34:5–7, KJV, emphasis added).

This is God's own definition of who He is. There are seven characteristics specified. He is *merciful, gracious, patient, good, truthful, forgiving,* and *just*. Because of our fallen nature and inborn fear and distrust of God, we have difficulty seeing Him and His character. Along with coming to save us, Jesus came to reveal the Father (see John 14:9). Because God's character is central in the controversy raging in the universe, Jesus came to show us what the Father is like.

My testimony is this: *He is as advertised in His Word!*

As you get to know Him by allowing Jesus into your heart, as you allow Jesus to be the center of your life, you will find Him to be trustworthy in every instance. You will see from my story how deeply involved Jesus wants to be in every area of your life. You will find that He is sovereign over everything—every circumstance, every situation. Every event is under His supervision, even on a busy university campus. He wants the best for us in every detail of our lives. You will have great peace if you come to believe that.

As we come ever closer to the last days, we seem to be confronted more and more by quandaries and confusion. Controversies involving the environment, political power, social issues, freedom, control, and the like, seem to have no clear answers and are dividing societies. Truth seems to be less and less of a standard. I believe this situation will worsen as the second coming approaches. Quandaries force difficult choices to be made. As these quandaries increase and confusion reigns, where can we find answers that will cut through the confusion and feed the soul?

In His wisdom, God has given us all that we need to know in the Bible. It is the Book of books. It is a Book of depth, wisdom, power, and love. It has endured the test of time because it satisfies the deepest longing of every heart. It takes in the heights and depths of human experience. And most of all, it reveals Jesus! Jesus, our Creator. Jesus, the Re-Creator of our hearts. Jesus, our savior, friend, and shepherd. Jesus is the focus from Genesis to Revelation.

"The creative energy that called the worlds into existence is in the Word of God. This Word imparts power; it begets life. Every command is a promise; accepted by the will, received into the soul, it brings with it the life of the Infinite One. It transforms the nature and re-creates the soul in the image of God" (White, *Education,* p. 126).

As you continue reading, you will see incontrovertible evidence that this statement is true. From the first time I, as an adult, picked it up, I experienced the power of the Bible to reveal my sinful nature and open my mind to my brokenness. It spoke directly to circumstances, revealed my need of a Savior, and brought healing into my life. It was an encounter so profound that my life was completely changed. The impact of this experience with God's power in the Word has never left me. No archaeological discovery, no argument from the evolutionists, no new thesis from the scientific community could challenge my *personal* encounter with God through His Word. The Holy Spirit has left an indelible imprint on my heart.

In the Bible is the wisdom of eternity, the comfort of a mother, views of the future, plans for life, encouragements, and warnings. Most important, the Bible reveals the great God of the universe and His one and only Son, Jesus (see John 1:14). Through the gentle yet powerful operation of the Holy Spirit, the Father and the Son go about bringing this world to a close and cleansing our hearts so we may live in His presence forever. He has given many tools in His Word to help us in this darkening world. Among the most helpful are the promises of God. There are literally thousands of promises in Scripture for us to lean on in good times and bad. They cover every area of life, both material and spiritual. The book *Christ's Object Lessons* comments, "And God stands back of every promise He has made" (White, p. 147). As you read, you will see how a crippled sinner like I, by claiming God's promises, can have the ability to traverse through life.

How do we access God's promises? Through the avenue of prayer. The heart of the Christian's life is prayer. It is the foundation for Bible study, fruitful service, and overcoming sin. Jesus said to the disciples in Gethsemane, "Watch and pray, lest you enter into temptation" (Matt. 26:41). Watching unto prayer is one of the most priceless gems in the Christian experience. Communing in the presence of God, sitting at His feet in the heavenly sanctuary, and sharing your heart are at the center of the Christian life. His heart's desire is to communicate with His children. One of the most significant outcomes from Jesus' sojourn in this world is that we can "come boldly [confidently] to the throne of grace, that we may obtain mercy and find grace to help in time of need" (Heb. 4:16).

My prayer is that, as you read my life story, with God writing it, you will be drawn closer to Him and that your faith in Jesus will grow. My hope is that you will expand your horizons concerning the role of the Bible in your daily life and the absolute privilege God has given us to commune with Him in prayer.

Remember: God is writing your life story, too!

1.

Painted Into a Corner

We've all heard the familiar expression about painting oneself into a corner. It describes a situation that you're stuck in (at least until the paint dries) as a result of your own actions. Mine was much worse than that; though I had prided myself on how well I could handle whatever came my way, and how I could accomplish whatever I needed to in order to take care of number one, I was now finding myself without the resources to handle what was going on in my life. I had painted myself into a corner and couldn't get out. Little did I know that God was using my dilemma to draw me to Himself, a surprise for a guy who, at the time, didn't even know that God existed!

I grew up in a secular family in Los Altos, California, in the San Francisco Bay area. It was a beautiful little town of apricot and plum orchards. At the time, it was a place where kids could ride their bikes anywhere and nobody locked their doors at night. Today it has been swallowed by the Silicon Valley. (Our family home, which my dad built for $20,000 in the early fifties, is valued

> *I had painted myself into a corner and couldn't get out.*

at $3.5 million today but would probably sell for twice as much.) America in the 1950s was a time when almost all Americans considered themselves Christian. So it was in my family, except that the daily Christian experience didn't exist. There was no talk about religion, no prayer in the home, no family worship, no *Uncle Arthur's Bedtime Stories,* and no Bible study. I don't remember ever seeing a Bible in our home, though there must have been one—somewhere (the attic, maybe?). Also, if there was church attendance, it would be sporadic, a Christmas, Thanksgiving, or Easter thing. I did not like going to any of them.

My parents, good, honest, mid-western stock, were faithful, hard-working citizens who grew up during the Great Depression. As such, they had little education and were highly focused on making a better life for my sister and me. Hammering and nailing for two hours a night after work and on weekends for over two years, my father built the house I grew up in. He had no building experience. My father was a milkman, back when there was home delivery. My mother worked for a doctor; this during a time when usually mothers didn't work. But my mother had to work to help maintain our lower middle-class status. I was a latchkey kid before the term had been coined. I ate more lunches at my friends' homes than at my place, because their mothers were there. Most of our neighbors were educated, successful, and secure. They were mostly pilots, college professors, electrical engineers, and doctors.

My sister was eight years older than I, so she had her own life. This led to a lonely childhood for me, which caused me to develop self-care skills that resulted in selfishness. I never chose to do anything that didn't benefit me in some way. The sinner's natural inclination is selfishness and self-sufficiency, and our current consumer-driven culture only feeds it.

My growing-up years were consumed with sports. I loved sports and all the teams and players and the competition. On Sundays, our gods were the San Francisco 49ers in the fall and the San Francisco Giants in the summer. I learned to read on the sports page. Everything came naturally to me in sports, and I was bigger and better than almost everyone. I focused on winning any competition I entered, and won many trophies and awards. One award I was particularly proud of was a county-wide football skills competition. My name was regularly in the local paper, *Los Altos News*. Being a low self-esteem family, we focused on our strengths rather than our weaknesses. My achievements gave our family a much-needed boost in the community.

Athletics was a benefit for me through my high school years, but it didn't help academically. After barely graduating from high school and entering junior college, I lost the edge I'd always had in competing; many players were now bigger and better than I was. Losing that long run of success, combined with immaturity, little interest in academics, and a growing interest in partying, led me to three academic failures.

It was, also, the 1960s, and the pull toward all that was happening—the Vietnam War, protesting, Haight-Ashbury, the hippy and rock music scene in San Francisco—was very strong. I dove headlong into the *zeitgeist,* the spirit of the day. Each of the three times I flunked out of school, I lost my student deferment. Draft notices followed. Three times I showed up for induction, and three times I was sent home, the last time with a 4F deferment due to an issue with my back. X-rays revealed that I had a defect in my lower back, the result of growing so fast as a kid. In my early twenties I would need major surgery to fix the problem.

With the deferment and the help of a new coach, I was somehow able to raise my grade point average just enough to be accepted into California State University at Chico. Looking back, I see that God was involved behind the scenes to make my college progress happen. Even when I didn't know He existed, He was watching over me and had a plan for my life!

I continued with a borderline academic record at Chico State until my last year. I had received a letter from the school stating that I needed a 3.4 grade average the following semester or I would be dropped from the program I was in. Three miracles happened that semester that enabled me to achieve the needed goal. God was looking out for me, again.

Upon graduating (barely), I made plans to travel to Mexico with a friend. The plans fell through, so I did the next best thing, back surgery. As long as I was in good physical condition playing sports, I had few problems, but once I got out of shape, I had increasing pain. One day I found myself crawling on the floor to get to the kitchen. That was the deciding factor. Most decisions have few consequences, but some have life-changing outcomes. This was one of the latter.

I did not know the severity of the surgery. Upon my moving back to my home at Los Altos, the doctor my mother worked for referred me to an expert orthopedist who pioneered the fusion procedure that I was needing. It was a long surgery, four and a half hours, and required five pints of blood. Back then they were still using "stone knives and bailing wire." I was in the hospital for two weeks; the recovery lasted one year. Those were hard days, for sure, especially for a guy who had been an uber athlete. Now, I could either lie down or walk with a large back brace.

About halfway through the year-long recovery, I moved back to Chico; while living there, I had met a young lady and her two kids, and we became close. She picked me up, and on the drive to her home I was stretched out in the back of her station wagon. As it turned out, that relationship played a pivotal role in my life.

Before the surgery, I had been involved in many socially unacceptable activities that I call "selfish crimes"—shop lifting, petty theft, minor drug sales, and flat-out lying. Fortunately, I was not a risk taker, and that kept me from grosser crimes. I would cut every corner I could in pursuit of saving money in order to be able to have what I wanted and to party harder. While recovering, I asked a friend to start a marijuana garden in our back yard. That yielded a handsome profit, a year of free pot, and a lot of paranoia.

This kind of activity was new to my girlfriend. Unknowingly, I was corrupting her life. I was living such a life that every event, decision, and action was governed by selfishness. Again, it all came back to number one.

I had no idea what this meant, but my girlfriend was a brand-new Seventh-day Adventist. When we first met, she was going through a messy divorce that, I think, had a part to play in her joining the church. She was a baby Christian, and I was unaware that my actions and decisions were disrupting her new beliefs. I did not understand that having me in her life caused a real conundrum. Looking back, I don't remember anyone from her church watching over her. So through my unconscious influence and the lack of support from the church, she was diverted in her infant walk with Jesus. Over the next couple of years, we continued our relationship, but I didn't realize that she was having struggles with her faith. I let her know that I had no interest in "church." It was simply not a part of my reality.

> *I was living such a life that every event, decision, and action was governed by selfishness. Again, it all came back to number one.*

One day, she declared that she wanted a Christian husband and wanted to break up. We were sitting in one our favorite spots on the front porch. I was devastated. I thought things were going pretty well. My obliviousness here shows how lacking in awareness and perspective I was at the time. I thought everything was all right, another way of saying that everything was going all right for *me*. I tried to change her mind, but her mind was made up. I had to move out.

Heartbroken, I moved across town to a small bungalow by some train tracks, with a friend from high school. The move was very emotional. I was shattered. I wasn't losing only my girlfriend, but also two kids I had come to love.

I began manifesting symptoms of psychological trouble. My emotional equilibrium was off. I felt as if I were being torn apart. I was the one who had always been in control of himself, and now I didn't know what to do except party harder. But that lifestyle brought little relief. When the anchors that have helped you through life begin to lose hold, it can be emotionally disrupting. My anchors were definitely unmoored, and I panicked.

After a few weeks, I started wondering if something was seriously wrong with me. But my pride and my do-it-on-my-own attitude kept me from moving in a positive direction—whatever that was. Relinquishing the hold that I'd had in running my life was not possible because of fear—fear of the unknown, fear of losing control, fear of the future. And I saw no way out. I was crushed and grieving.

As time passed and things didn't get any better, I decided to see my girlfriend, thinking that might help (and hoping she might take me back). Up to that point, I hadn't confided in anyone about these issues. We had a strange conversation at the kitchen table; it was very uncomfortable. It was as if we didn't know each other very well. She avoided talking about "us." I did most of the talking. She said almost nothing. It was as if her mouth was barred from moving. At the end of the conversation, she simply said, "I don't know what to say." I left dissatisfied and headed back to the darkening dungeon that my little bungalow had become.

The situation had become unrelenting. I couldn't find relief. I had been isolating for the most part, so I decided to start seeing friends and participating in social activities like sporting events at the university, and going to parties, movies and bars. But my dysfunction only increased. I felt detached and uncomfortable around my friends. What is happening to me? I started wondering if I needed to see a doctor. No, I don't need anyone's help. I didn't know it, but there was no help, no activity, no doctor's cure, no treatment the world could offer. So I suffered alone. *Alone.* What a simple word that spoke volumes about my situation. It reminded me of how I felt at times growing up as a latchkey kid. Alone then, alone now.

The autumn leaves had fallen. The holiday season was coming, but I wasn't improving. Maybe this was my "new normal." Usually, people adjust to new situations after a while. I didn't. Today my situation would be categorized as an adjustment disorder or as features of post-traumatic stress disorder. Had the trauma of the breakup been *that* disruptive to my emotional system? Something I saw on television caused me to wonder if, maybe, I were depressed. But as usual, I dismissed such an idea, not wanting to admit that I needed help. Things, I told myself, would get better.

Things did not. In fact, they got worse. I visited my girlfriend again, hoping she would invite me to her parents' house for Thanksgiving. But she said that she wasn't going to her parents' this year. Our conversation was much the same as before: I talked, she listened. I told her I felt that I was carrying a heavy burden and that life was closing in on me. Once again, she said, "I don't know what to say." She ended our conversation by telling me she had to go because a "friend" was coming to visit. I knew what that meant, and left with a fresh wound in my heart. I knew she was seeing someone, because one day I had seen her coming out of an ice cream shop and getting into a red truck.

Would the pain ever stop?

A couple of incidents that took place right outside my bungalow brought in a new element of disruption—they were sheer craziness. The bungalow was situated on a curve, close to a long, narrow rural road. From my front window, I could see cars coming from a long way off. The positioning was such that it looked as if the cars were coming directly at the bungalow before swinging at the last moment to the left and going up and over the railroad tracks, which were about twenty-five yards away. I was partying with a friend one night when I noticed a car heading toward us on the road. I could tell from experience that the car, a large station wagon, was moving very fast and, as usual, looked like it would run right into the bungalow. But as the car approached the curve, I could tell it wasn't going to make it. With tires screeching, it didn't quite navigate the curve and it hit, with a dull thud, headlong into the concrete post that protected the crossing guard.

Inebriated, we ran out the door into what looked like a sudden snowstorm. Papers, what looked like a thousand of them, were floating in the air. The car had been packed with boxes of paper that went sailing on impact. The amber streetlight, combined with our distorted perception, created an eerie atmosphere. Being the first on the scene of an accident was very strange. As we approached, I went to the driver's side, my friend to the other. I looked in the shattered window only to find that there wasn't anybody there. In shock, I didn't understand what that meant. We both heard groaning from in front of the car. Upon checking, we found the driver lying on the ground. There was blood everywhere. It was gruesome. The driver had been thrown through the windshield and the top of his scalp sheared off, tomahawk style. All this gore, combined with what I was already dealing with emotionally? I was ready to go off the edge.

Fortunately, right then, someone appeared—out of thin air it seemed—and pressed a sweatshirt onto the man's head. Shaking off the shock, we ran back to the house to call the police. There were no cell phones or 911 services back then. So, distraught, we stayed inside and let those who seemed to know what to do, take care of things. We gave a statement to the police. I never heard what happened to the driver, but even if he lived, I can't imagine he would ever be the same. This trauma added more disruption to my life. The effects of the grisly accident only increased my condition. I became more distrustful, more distant from others, and anxious.

As if a horrific car wreck outside my house weren't enough, there was a train derailment right outside my bedroom window a few days later. The tracks were about twenty yards from my room. Every morning around three o'clock a train would pass by. I had gotten used to the noise and would usually return to my slumber. Up to this point, sleep was the one positive thing in my life. I looked forward to going to bed, as it was an escape from my emotional difficulties. I slept soundly and was unhappy when it was time wake up. This particular night I was having trouble sleeping. As I tossed and turned, I heard the train approaching. Since there was a crossing right there, the train would pass slowly. I was accustomed to the brakes, the steam, and the creaking sounds from the cars. But suddenly there was an ear-piercing screech followed by the sound of iron on iron, and whistles blowing. The bungalow was shaking. The screeching noise sounded like a pack of banshees coming through the window to announce my death. I never found out what caused the derailment, but the train was stuck. Though not tipped over or anything like that, it was off the tracks and it blocked the crossing into the following afternoon. If the train had been going any faster, it would have taken out our little bungalow.

She didn't say a word, but she handed me a small stack of books, turned, and disappeared into the storm.

Though the banshee attack was imaginary, the fear it caused was real and it kept me up for the rest of the night. I was worn to a frazzle and my thoughts about getting help re-emerged. But the resolve to handle things on my own was still there. Stubbornness is a trait of the fallen nature. I had this problem, big time. To acknowledge need was beyond my ability. To admit to need was not a part of my existence; I saw it as a weakness.

As winter was in the air, a pivotal event occurred. In the middle of a heavy rainstorm, there was a knock on the door. As I opened the door, I was shocked to see my girlfriend standing there. She didn't say a word, but she handed me a small stack of books, turned, and disappeared into the storm. I stood there, stunned, looking into the dark. After a minute or two, I closed the door and, without looking at the books, put them down on a table. I spent the rest of the evening contemplating what had just happened, and why. Was this an opening gesture on her part, to get back together? Why had she come out in the rainstorm? Did it have any significance at all? Late into the night, I finally went into a deep sleep.

Eventually I looked at what she left me. The stack contained a Bible, a book called *The Great Controversy*, a book entitled *Your Bible and You*, a Bible-study set called *Twentieth-Century Bible Studies,* and several pamphlets. Little did I know then that the greatest power in the universe, the only true healing power, the answer to all my problems, were all there on a little table in my bungalow. But, not knowing that, I left the books to sit there as I continued to suffer. It turned cold in November, and the winter of my life was upon me.

Out of nowhere, I began to have sleep issues. Lack of sleep will, of course, aggravate any problem, and it certainly did mine. The increase in my emotional upheaval was almost more than I could bear. The depression that I was denying only deepened without sleep. The one positive aspect of my life was disrupted. Even going to bed was something I could no longer look forward to. Any kind of hopeful outlook was gone.

Where is my life going? Am I always going to be like this? Is there any way out?

But as difficult as it was, my stubbornness and the need to control continued to win the day. What else did I have? But with my own choices, I was painting myself into a corner. And I didn't know it!

The sleepless nights took on an evil, spiritual dimension. I felt harassed and oppressed. (How could I have known then that the mere presence of those books would cause a satanic attack as the enemy tried to keep me from Jesus, no matter what?) I couldn't find a comfortable position. At times I would be hot or cold. There were swishing sounds, like a noisy old fan on low speed. I didn't know what to think. I'd certainly had some bizarre experiences back in the sixties, but never anything like this. This was different. There was some authority, some power involved, and it was disconcerting. I could sense it. Without sleep, my days were rough. I was in a kind of stupor. An endless malaise. The world seemed to exist only in shades of gray.

I wasn't working at the time, so I had little responsibility. It was fortunate because I wouldn't have been able to do a reasonable job, I think, at anything. Each night was an adventure. I would stay up as late as possible, hoping that when I went to bed, the fatigue would put me to sleep. This situation culminated one night when I was wrestling with sleep. I heard rapping on my closet door. I didn't know what to think. The atmosphere in the room was heavy as I went to check the door. Everything seemed normal in my closet, so I just dismissed it along with the other strange events of the previous few months. I went out to the living room looking for something to do to put me to sleep.

For some reason, I was drawn to *The Great Controversy*. I began reading and found it mildly interesting. The first chapter concerns Jesus' prophesying to the disciples about the coming destruction of Jerusalem. After several pages, I felt drowsy and went to bed. Instantly I fell into a deep sleep.

Another abysmal week went by with no change in my condition. The days passed slowly, with the distress and craziness continuing. I wasn't thinking about the next day, let alone the next week. Thanksgiving was right around the corner and hadn't entered my thoughts. Then my room-mate told me he would be leaving the following day to be with his parents for Thanksgiving.

Thanksgiving! What a shock. I had made no plans. I quickly called several friends only to find that they had plans or had already left for the holiday. It hit me hard: *I was going to be alone on Thanksgiving.* Alone again.

I woke up to a cold, dreary Thanksgiving morning. Just another dismal day in my crazy life. The Macy's Thanksgiving Parade on television held no interest for me. For the first time in my life, one of my favorite activities, watching football, didn't draw me. I found myself sitting in the living room looking at the little fireplace and realizing how cold it was. But I had no wood to start a fire. Then I remembered that when I was living with my girlfriend, I had cut up a fallen limb in her backyard. Since she didn't have a fireplace, I figured she wouldn't mind if I came by and took some of the wood. I jumped into my car and drove the mile or so to her home.

As I stood there, I felt as if I had taken a gunshot to my heart.

The first thing I noticed as I entered her driveway was that her car was gone; that was for the better. It would cause me less pain not to see her. As I got out of the car, I noticed a red truck parked in front of her house. The same truck that I had seen her in earlier. That stunned me. It could mean only one of two things. Either she had changed her mind and asked her new friend to go to her parents' home, or she had lied to me.

Something happened, right there in her driveway, something I have never forgotten. Something so real, so painful, so dynamic. As I stood there, I felt as if I had taken a gunshot to my heart. Right there in the driveway, I broke down, wailing, screaming at the top of my lungs. Tears were pouring down my cheeks. Forgetting the firewood, I stumbled into my car and, somehow, drove home safely. I was out of control. It had been years, maybe decades, since I had cried. And here I was, wailing, a basket case. I was having a catharsis, a release of strong or repressed emotions.

As I arrived home, I stumbled out of my car and through the front door. I was still in the throes of this emotional breakdown. It wasn't letting up. It was more than just the current situation. A torrent of tears from years of pent-up frustration, fear, and disappointment were pouring down my cheeks. I plopped down in the nearest chair and just cried. Sitting on the little table next to the chair was the stack of books. I wondered if there might be something there to help me. One of the only things I knew about God was that He was supposed to help people.

Still hurting, still crying uncontrollably, I picked up the book *Your Bible and You,* a general book about the Bible. Looking down the table of contents, my eye stopped at a chapter called, "Why So Much Suffering?" Still crying, I turned to that chapter, which had a Bible verse under the chapter title. It was Lamentations 3:33, which said, *"For He does not afflict willingly, Nor grieve the children of men."* I decided to try to find that verse, so I picked up the Bible. For the first time as a discerning adult, I held the greatest, most powerful book ever written. Having no idea how to find a verse, I just opened it. To my amazement, I opened right to Lamentations 3. Astoundingly, I began looking for verse 33, when a physical presence pulled my eyes across the page, to the beginning of the chapter. And the first seven verses read,

> I am the man who has seen the afflictions that come from the rod of God's wrath. He has brought me into deepest darkness, shutting out all light. He has turned against me. Day and night his hand is heavy on me. He has made me old and has broken my bones. He has built forts against me and surrounded me with anguish and distress. He buried me in dark places, like those long dead. He has walled me in; I cannot escape; he has fastened me with heavy chains. (TLB)

At this point, I was beside myself, still crying with the emotional upheaval, and not quite comprehending what was happening. Then a voice within me said, *This is your experience. This is what you've been going through.* My next thought was, How could a book so old know what I have been going through? This is insanity.

I started reading the passage again. As I would come to a verse that seemed to apply to me, the words, along with the verse number would come up off the page and get bigger and bigger and bigger and go into my mind. I wondered if I was going crazy. Was I having flashbacks from my use of hallucinogens in the sixties? But no, this was too real. Verse 5, which talked about "surrounding me with anguish and distress," flew into my mind. Then verse 7, which talked about being "walled in" and "fastened with heavy chains," flashed me back to the time that I had told my girlfriend that I was carrying a heavy burden and life was closing in on me.

How could this book know these things? What was going on? Then, finally, I came to verses 12 and 13, which said, "He has bent His bow and aimed it squarely at me and sent His arrows deep within my heart." I flashed back to just a few minutes earlier when, in my girlfriend's driveway, I felt as if I had been shot in the heart. This was too much! I couldn't take it anymore. Through anguished tears I found myself crying out, "Help me! Help me!"

Once again, I sobbed and sobbed. I never knew someone could have so many tears. Wiping my eyes, I was again directed to the Scripture. My eyes moved over to the next column and fell on verses 21–26:

> *Yet there is one ray of hope: his compassion never ends.* It is only the Lord's mercies that have kept us from complete destruction. Great is his faithfulness; his loving-kindness begins afresh each day. My soul claims the Lord as my inheritance; therefore, I will hope in him. The Lord is wonderfully good to those who wait for him, to those who seek for him. It is good both to hope and wait quietly for the salvation of the Lord. (TLB)

Then I felt a gentle hand rest on my shoulder. I looked but no one was there. Wow, what now! I was in turmoil. What was happening? My feet turned hot, really hot. Then a band of heat started moving slowly up my body, to my calves, my thighs, my waist, my chest, and up to and out of my head. I was thrown onto the floor and I yelled something like *take me* or *I'm yours*. In that moment, I was healed. I knew it instantly, too. I was healed! No more depression. No more oppression. No more craziness. I lay there and laughed and laughed. At twenty-seven years of age, I had met my Savior!

Not fully understanding all that was going on, I knew that something dynamic had occurred because, again—*I was healed*. As the Bible says

"Therefore, if anyone *is* in Christ, he *is* a new creation; old things have passed away; behold, all things have become new" (2 Cor. 5:17).

> *Also, because I had no previous background in the Bible, there wasn't anything to unlearn or challenge with a previous understanding.*

It wasn't just the healing, either. Everything had changed. Colors seemed brighter, noises seemed sharper, my step was lighter, and my taste was sharper. I cleaned out the refrigerator and had the best Thanksgiving meal ever—three eggs and hash browns. It tasted as if it had come from the Garden of Eden itself. Over the next few days, friends greeted me with, "What happened to you?" When my roommate returned a couple of days later, he said the same thing. I told him what had happened, and about a month later, he gave himself to the Lord.

I now had an unquenchable thirst for the Bible. I dove into the set of Bible studies that my girlfriend had given me, and went through them twice, as quickly as I could. I had no background in Bible doctrine but, in God's mercy, He gave me an abundance of grace to understand what I had been reading. Also, because I had no previous background in the Bible, there wasn't anything to unlearn or challenge with a previous understanding. I was a clean slate, a dry sponge. If the Bible said it, I believed it. Doctrines about the Sabbath, the state of the dead, the tithe, and the second coming, I easily accepted. Others, like the prophecies, came with time.

I truly had been born again. No question, I had "painted myself into a corner," a corner that only God could have gotten me out of. And He did—and I, now and forever, will be grateful.

2.

The Church at Chico

The following day, I called my girlfriend. I must have sounded like a babbling fool, talking frantically, nonstop. I described a little of what had happened. My ecstasy knew no bounds. I had met Jesus and He healed me! I know she must have been stunned, wondering what was going on.

What happened? Has he lost his mind? Is this just a story? Is he just trying to get back with me?

She allowed me a visit. I was excited to tell my story and see her reaction. I came over just like I used to when we were first getting acquainted. It was winter, so we sat together in her living room. She didn't know how to react to my conversion story. I thought it was a great visit, and left feeling very good. Nothing had changed about our relationship but, somehow, that didn't seem to be a high priority anymore. I had kind of died to it, which, I supposed, was what had to have happened. It was all part of the healing process.

The ensuing days were filled with Bible study. Sometimes I would get through three lessons at a sitting. I had never been so happy, so content. I was being fed with spiritual food. The Bible was fascinating, uplifting, and powerful. I was learning, day by day. I was learning about the central role of Jesus, about His atoning death on my behalf, and about how all of my sins have been forgiven and that I could stand, even now, perfect in the sight of God. That, despite all I had done, despite all that I was. God loved me, and I was accepted through Jesus. I, truly, was born again.

I was overwhelmed by all the Bible taught. The power and depth of the Word is summarized in one of my favorite verses, Hebrews 4:12: "For the Word of God *is* living and powerful, and sharper than any two-edged sword, piercing even to the division of soul and spirit, and of joints and marrow, and is a discerner of the thoughts and intents of the heart." Dissecting and contemplating this verse as best I could, gave me a deeper insight into the role of the Bible in my sanctification. It is an essential part

of my walk with Jesus. The book *Education* makes this remarkable statement about the power of the Bible:

> The creative energy that called the worlds into existence is in the
> word of God. This word imparts power; it begets life. Every com-
> mand is a promise; accepted by the will, received into the soul, it
> brings with it the life of the Infinite One. It transforms the nature
> and re-creates the soul in the image of God. (White, p. 126)

It transforms the nature and re-creates the soul in the image of God.
Praise God! That's what happened to me. A wretched sinner re-created
in the image of God. Though all of this was new to me, and I didn't fully
understand it (and still don't), all I knew was that the Word of God was
transforming me into a new being.

Shortly after my conversion, I considered going to church. But the
thought made me anxious, so I put it off. I hadn't walked through a church
door since I was a child, and that left me with some negative vibes. Also,
with my height, reddish brown "Bozo" hair and full beard, I knew I would
be a spectacle at any church. What would they do with me?

In my new understanding of the Sabbath, I knew that I would go to a
Sabbath-keeping church. Eventually, I decided to attend the Chico church
the following Saturday. God went before me and prepared the way. It is
incredible how God can arrange events, sometimes years ahead, so as to
dovetail them into His plan for someone. Here is what happened.

A couple of years before my conversion, I took a summer school
course on the psychology of prejudice, at Chico State. The professor was a
tall man with long hair and a beard. He
looked like pictures of Jesus. I enjoyed
his class and received a good grade,
which helped me graduate.

> *God can arrange
> events, sometimes
> years ahead, so as
> to dovetail them into
> His plan for someone.*

I finally got up the nerve to go to
church. I had an old rust-colored corduroy suit that I hadn't worn in years.
Amazingly, it still fit (a bit tight around
the middle, though). As I arrived at the church, I noticed a large building
project was in progress; they were building a church complex, and so the
congregation was meeting in the school gymnasium. This lessened some
of the formality for me. I could better relate to a gym than to a church.

As I anxiously walked up to the entryway, I was stunned to see my
summer school professor greeting people at the door. I recognized him

immediately, and he recognized me. My comfort level rose. We chatted briefly and he said he had some duties to take care of. During the worship service, he was on the platform. He was one of the elders. He later became one of my mentors. Did I not see the hand of God in this? Of course. Imagine, instead of seeing him, who instantly gave me some good vibes, I had seen a teacher or a professor whose mere presence was a turn-off?

I again visited my girlfriend and told her that it didn't matter whether we got back together or not; either way, I sensed that Jesus was calling me to be a Seventh-day Adventist. We had an affable time together and I left. Over the coming weeks and months, we spent more time together, but only in an agreed-upon "new Christian relationship." This was new to us both, but things seemed to go smoothly.

We started attending church together occasionally. The members of the church were wonderful. I don't think they knew what to do with someone like me. It was the mid-seventies, the church was conservative; my persona, my laisse-faire view of life, informal attire—everything about me was out of their comfort zone. But they loved me anyway. It was a new experience for me; I felt awkward the first few times we attended, but over time I felt better and better being there.

After a few weeks, some realities started setting in. Though I was a changed man, "born again," some lifestyle issues reared their ugly heads. God can change a heart—even overnight. But the reality is that any change is the result of a preparation process that only God understands. A process that takes time because God is dealing with our freedom of choice, our humanness, the whole of a sin-damaged and sin-distorted life. God knows our frailties, knows that we are dust (see Ps. 103:14.) He is amazing in His dealing with the very inner recesses of a heart. It took even the Creator of the universe, time to gently manipulate the changes to my soul. Some changes can be made easily; others are deeply rooted and take time because we are so corrupt and because He does not force the will.

For me, a few things dropped away immediately. One was my foul mouth. The s-word was my favorite word. I used it to describe good and bad. Being in the company of Christians now, I knew that this crass habit had to go. That was the most obvious thing God healed at my conversion.

At the time, I really didn't know anything about this transformation process. So I was taken aback when some lifestyle issues appeared, some thoughts and habits a Christian shouldn't have. I didn't know what to do with these things I knew I shouldn't be thinking or doing. What was going on? Was I really even saved? At times I wondered. At those moments all I could do was claim the Gospel promises of forgiveness and acceptance in Jesus. Jesus was perfect, and I am perfect in Him, in His righteousness—a truth that I had to cling to as best I could.

I grasped, only dimly, how merciful and forgiving God is; how patient He is with my frailties. 1 John 1:9 is one of my most-claimed promises: "If we confess our sins, He is faithful and just to forgive us *our* sins and to cleanse us from all unrighteousness." There is no limitation on that promise, no deadline. Jesus offers me His righteous robe to cover my sin and enable me to overcome. It is comforting to realize that when I go before the judgment, Jesus and His righteousness will take my place. He has the power to get me to where He wants me to be. My part is to cooperate with the work of the Holy Spirit in my walk with Him. The key is not to let my faults and shortcomings discourage me, which is easy to do.

As spring was approaching, my girlfriend and I were having a good time in our "new relationship." So good, in fact, that we decided to get married. It seemed like the next step in our lives. After talking about it and making a decision, we set a date. I was thrilled. I went to the church to talk with the pastor about marrying us. The church construction was still in progress and I had to ask around to find the pastor. In the few times I had attended, I hadn't met him. Upon finding him, I was amused that he was dressed in construction gear. At the time, the parallel between the pastor being a carpenter and the Master Carpenter escaped me.

When I told him why I was there, he asked me if I was a baptized member of the SDA church. When I said no, he kindly informed me that he could marry members of the church only. This led to a discussion about what needed to happen before he could marry us. It was easy for me to decide to be baptized.

I had no understanding about any requirements; I was just thrilled that I had met Jesus. I told the pastor about my conversion and my relationship with my fiancée. We decided to meet three times a week for Bible study, in order to prepare for baptism. The date we had set was just a few weeks away. I knew nothing about the "qualifications" for joining the church and the process I had to follow.

But it didn't matter. Whatever I had to do was okay with me. The studies went well with the pastor. He was amazed at how much I already knew of SDA doctrine. I didn't really understand at the time that this packet of Bible studies that I had been using had, actually, been built around Seventh-day Adventist doctrine.

A big weekend was planned. I was to be baptized on Sabbath afternoon and married the next day. I was happy that everything fell together,
after my fiancée and I had made the premature plans. Looking back, I
realize I should have gone a bit more slowly in these decisions. But at the
time, I wasn't one for patience. I had met Jesus and I was ready to move
full speed ahead in my new life. What I should have done was wait on the
marriage and find out what it meant to be a Christian and to be a member of the Seventh-day Adventist church. The events of the previous few
months were massive changes for me. Massive!

And to top it all off, I get married?

The Sabbath arrived and I had completed the studies with the pastor. I was baptized on Sabbath afternoon in the old downtown SDA
church. I was amazed so many people
would come to see someone they didn't
know get baptized. There was music
and prayer. I have to admit I was a little disappointed. I had no idea what was
going to happen as I hit the water. After
my conversion experience I expected
lightning or something. When nothing
happened except a lot of *amens,* I was
a little let down, but happy nonetheless.
The important thing was that I had met

> *I doubt many
> new Christians
> understand what the
> Christian walk is
> going to be—what it
> means to respond to
> the call of Jesus.*

Jesus, and I publicly announced it by being baptized. The following day we
had a small wedding in the fireside room, just off the gymnasium. I bought
a new suit to replace the old corduroy one. And my sister saved the day.
Ever the organizer, she stepped in at the last minute to set up the punch
and hors d'oeuvres when the person who was supposed to do it ended up
sick. Relatives and friends attended. It was, all and all, a great experience,
a happy day for me.

Truly, I had a whole new life: a wife, two step kids, and a new job that
God provided. I was hired to manage a new commercial recreation business located in a fancy new mall not far from where we lived.

Yet there was also the reality of selfishness and the adversary of our
souls. Though I knew I had a changed heart and a new start, I found rather
quickly that there was an enemy. As soon as our honeymoon ended, my
honeymoon with Jesus ended also.

I doubt many new Christians understand what the Christian walk is
going to be—what it means to respond to the call of Jesus. I didn't. Ours

was a marriage of two baby Christians. We both made mistakes and took lots of missteps right from the start. Looking back, I see that many of the things I did that I thought were right, were wrong. Navigating through marriage was not easy for us. We both brought a great deal of brokenness to the union. Anything that is broken doesn't work right. And that sums up our marriage. But even with things working against us, there were also good times. A highlight was that we were able to put an addition onto our little house, which gave the kids their own rooms. Despite all that was coming, we had some really good times together as a family, and I thank God for it.

About two years after we were married, something happened that revealed God's working in my life. My parents loved my wife from the beginning. But they didn't like that I had become an Adventist. My mother had gone to the library and checked out a book that had one chapter on various churches. She didn't like what she read. This led to some bitterness when we were together as, at times, she mocked my faith. So however painful, I decided to limit the number of events we attended with my parents.

Easter Sunday was coming. We had no plans to visit my parents. But the Wednesday before that weekend I woke up early, with a strong feeling that we were supposed to go see them. I woke my wife and told her. I talked to God about our going, asking for the blessing of a harmonious Easter weekend.

In advance of the weekend, we made two important decisions. First, we wouldn't upset my parents by going to church or making a big fuss about eating in a restaurant on the Sabbath; at times we infuriated them with this "Jewish stuff." Second, we would let the kids participate in an Easter egg hunt at my sister's the next morning, despite our being aware of just how pagan the whole thing was. Even though my parents weren't church-going people, Easter was a big holiday for them. After dinner we would go to my parents' home for dessert. My sister and her kids would be there as well, making it more fun for my step kids. It promised to be a good time.

The plan was for our family to go to my sister's house on Saturday night so the kids could have their egg hunt in the morning. My parents would join us as soon as they could. So that night, we drove the thirty minutes to my sister's. About fifteen minutes after we arrived, my sister took a phone call. I could see in her face that something was up. She quietly gave me the phone. A policeman was on the other end. All he would tell me was that

I needed to go back to my parents' home. I tried to get some information, but he told me again that I needed to come. I had a strange foreboding as I drove on the freeway. When I arrived, there were a couple of police cars in front of the house. I dashed in and found my dad stretched out on the kitchen floor. He'd had a massive heart attack and died.

I was stunned and went to check on my mother. She was in shock and didn't realize I was there. So I went back to the kitchen and talked with the police officer. I asked if I could be alone with my dad. I closed the door and knelt down next to his body. He looked asleep, so serene and at peace. His graying hair was still soft, and I found myself gently resting a hand on his shoulder. In my baby faith, I asked God to heal him. But it wasn't to be.

Death is, we know, an unfortunate reality, perhaps the most unfortunate reality in this fallen world. And though questions remain, how thankful I am to God that He is involved in every aspect of my life. Had He not directed me to come visit for Easter—despite my misgivings about spending time with my family in general, and the holiday in particular—I would not have had that one last moment with Dad. I am so grateful.

3.

Chastened by the Spirit

The narrow vision of a sinner such as myself makes it difficult to be a good spouse. My vision was narrower, I think, than most people's, and that made it tough to meet my spouse's needs. To put the other person first is one of the most important of the commandments for the Christian, and it is particularly important in a marriage. Selfishness is at the root of all problems, especially in a marriage. I wasn't very good at being a husband. My wife was probably better as a spouse, but as a citizen of this fallen world, she had her failings and weaknesses, too.

In short, we struggled for seven years before the adversary got the upper hand. We allowed him into our marriage through lifestyle issues we never let go of; that, and our own selfish choices doomed us from the start. Also, we were lax in our family spiritual life. All things considered, a split was inevitable. Not a matter of *if* but of *when*, unfortunately.

We decided to go our separate ways. I found myself looking for an apartment to move to, which led to another crazy, emotional, yet blessed, experience with the Lord.

Because we were in a college town, there wasn't an abundance of vacant housing, but God was merciful. He had gone before me once again. After a short search, He provided the most inexpensive but furnished apartment in Chico. It was just what I needed. It was on the other side of town, far from the student section, in a secluded area, tucked behind a Chinese restaurant. I was amazed when I realized that God knew every apartment in town and how to lead me to it.

Moving out was not easy. It was very emotional. The deep, spiritual/ emotional bond created by "becoming one flesh" is real. It reaches to the very core of our being. When that bond is torn, it hurts deeply. When a couple says their *I dos*, they become one flesh, spiritually and emotionally. So once again, I was on an emotional roller coaster. At least this time I had the knowledge that God was with me. I was about to find out again how much I needed Him. And about how powerful, merciful, and caring He is.

I continued going to church occasionally. It was strange and awkward, wondering what people were thinking. Did they notice that I was alone? It was difficult. Fortunately, the church was large, so it was easy to be anonymous and just kind of disappear. For some reason, I decided to visit the church library one Sabbath after worship. My eyes were drawn to the set of *Testimonies for the Church* (White), bound in red, on the shelf. I hadn't spent much time with them in my seven years of walking with the Lord. I was more acquainted with the series *Conflict of the Ages*.

I decided to check out two volumes at a time until I had read the set of nine books. I didn't know what I was getting myself into. I believe, based on my experience, that the *Testimonies* should be handled very carefully and prayerfully. They shouldn't be read traditionally, from front to back. These testimonies are powerful and, to get the most of what God wants us to get from them, we need to read them in God's timing, in the order that He leads. Reading a personal, powerful testimony when someone is not ready for it, or that wasn't written for them, can be overwhelming.

I was unfamiliar with these books, so I found myself checking out the table of contents in Volume 1 and reading a few testimonies. Interesting stuff, but it didn't seem to have much impact on my life.

Volume 2 was a different story. I was directed to two separate chapters over a few hours one Sabbath afternoon. The first one was written to a man who didn't know what real love was. The second told me, even though it had been written before I was born (that's the power of these books), that I didn't know how to love my wife.

Have you ever been chastened by The Holy Spirit? It hurts in more ways and more deeply than any physical discipline could. I knew immediately that God was speaking to me through these words. And it hurt! It went to the core of my being. When the Holy Spirit opens your mind and heart, you learn in a way that is difficult to describe. All defense mechanisms, all cultivated thought habits, all natural tendencies, all inhibitions, all opinions, are swept away in a moment. Anything that would hinder the understanding of God is removed.

When I see myself standing there, in the shame of my moral and spiritual nakedness, in my own moral and spiritual poverty, it is overwhelming and emotionally painful. The nakedness represents my self-righteousness and all worldly devices I use to get through the pain of this life. Seeing the truth about myself, in the clarity of the Holy Spirit, is not something that my *self* wants to happen. The self does not want to be discovered; it wants to be in control and, even worse, it wants to lie to me about what I am really like.

One of my favorite devotionals, *Thoughts from the Mount of Blessing*, makes this insightful statement: "Selfishness and pride will make a stand against anything that would show them to be sinful" (White, p. 141). However shameful and painful this experience, it was what I needed, and it dropped me to my knees in my little room. That's the best place we can be, on our knees, our souls open and exposed to God, from whom nothing is hidden.

God was merciful in waiting a couple of days before hitting me with a third testimony. As my heart was already hurting from the previous testimonies, this one completely tore my heart. God showed me that I had a big pride problem. Pride is the essence of the adversary's weapons. Basically, pride says *I have no need of God*.

This is a basic problem of the fallen human condition. That's why we desperately need Jesus and the new heart that He wants to give us. Pride is deceptive. It tells us a complete falsehood. The truth is, we need God for every breath we take and for every beat of our heart. He is not just the Creator but the Sustainer, the one in whom "we live and move and have our being" (Acts 17:28). Pride is the antithesis of the truth about our need for God. That's why God lists *pride* first in the list of the sins He hates the most (see Prov. 6:16–19).

There seem to be two categories of pride. With the first, a person is so gifted that they seem to handle every situation in life. They seem to walk a half inch off the ground. It is very difficult for them to see their need of God. The second type is like me. These persons feel so poorly about themselves that they spend a great deal of energy covering the feeling of inadequacy and making themselves look good to others.

After being chastened again by the Holy Spirit, I found myself on my knees and crying out to God. One of the main reasons God reveals sin to me is to get me to enter into His presence through prayer. For His presence is comforting, soothing, safe, healing, and the best place to find grace in our time of need.

"Let us therefore come boldly [confidently, with assurance] to the throne of grace, that we may obtain mercy, and find grace in our time of need" (Heb. 4:16). I needed mercy, I needed forgiveness, I needed comfort, safety, and healing. I needed all of that—desperately.

The next day I had to go to work; weary, torn, emotional. I was still managing the busy commercial recreation business, and didn't look forward to encountering customers and completing taking care of responsibilities. I did not know what the day was going to be like. It wasn't one of my better days. Every couple of hours, I had to leave the floor and go into my office and cry out to God. This continued through the week. I would find myself at the end of the day running to my truck. And when I got home, I would immediately fall on my knees, with my Bible.

This happened for days. Sometimes I would be there long enough that it would be dark when I realized where I was. Where had I been? I knew I had been in God's presence. It was strange times, but I surmised that God was working in my heart again. Many nights I would go to sleep clutching my Bible. Several times during this period God tested me to my limit. I would be lying on my bed reading and suddenly I would feel great inner turmoil, which would increase to the point where I would be flopping on the bed like a fish out of water. I would cry out to God for it to stop. Sooner or later, it would stop.

Also, during this time I experienced a considerable weight loss, without trying. It seemed as if God was doing some reconstruction in my soul, which, indeed, can have an impact on the body. How it all works, who knows? I know only that it works. The intensity at work and home dissipated as time went by, much to my joy. God was working with me; I knew it, but I needed a break.

As time passed, things seemed to settle down and a somewhat normal life returned. I found myself naturally taking God more seriously. Through all the recent trials, Jesus had become more real to me, more tangible, more precious. This seemed to be the blessed result of going through trials.

Unfortunately, some trials, temptations, and tests are a way of life in our fallen world and will happen as a matter of course. Then there are those trials that we bring on ourselves. I seem to do myself in, and on a regular basis, through my poor choices. If taken with the right attitude, however, trials that come from God can be among our greatest blessings.

God is not like us; He doesn't make mistakes. The apostle Paul went through many trials. They led to spiritual growth and dynamic ministry. Spiritual growth is the most coveted achievement for the Christian. It seems, though, that the road to that growth is through trial. James summarized the road to spiritual growth. "My brethren, count it all joy when you fall into various trials, knowing that the testing of your faith produces patience. But let patience have *its* perfect work, that you may be perfect and complete, lacking nothing" (James 1:2–4).

I can't get around it; if I want to be like Jesus, I will have to walk some of the same roads He did. And I know where that led. It is the greatest privilege for the Christian to walk as Jesus walked. With Jesus, no trial or temptation is wasted. He allows only that which is for my good. Every trial comes to Him first. He checks it out and determines whether the trial, if taken in faith, will benefit the person. How that process works in real time I have no idea. But I believe it. Praise Jesus! If you truly believe that, you will have much peace.

Thoughts from the Mount of Blessing presents this tremendous picture: "The Father's presence encircled Christ, and nothing befell Him but that which infinite love permitted for the blessing of the world. Here was His source of comfort, and *it is for us.* He who is imbued with the Spirit of Christ abides in Christ. The blow that is aimed at him falls upon the Savior, who surrounds him with His presence. Whatever comes to him comes from Christ. He has no need to resist evil, for Christ is his defense. Nothing can touch him except by our Lord's permission" (p.71).

My—what an incredible picture of Jesus, and how comforting for me as I travel through this fallen world! Jesus took, for us, whatever the adversary threw at Him while He was in this world. And He continues to take those arrows for us, even though He allows trials that will benefit our spiritual growth.

Coming from a secular background, I continued to struggle with lifestyle issues. Some long-established habits take time for true healing to occur. Only God knows when He can reach into a person's soul and bring complete healing. This happened to me on Sunday, March 27, 1983.

One of my struggles had been with marijuana. As a child of the sixties, I, like many others, had gotten caught in the web the adversary was spinning at the time. For many years, it was simply a part of my lifestyle. My conversion made inroads to this soul-defiling habit, but it didn't eradicate it. Jesus let me know early in my newly-changed life that I needed to overcome. The battle ensued, with many victories, some defeats. It seems that the level of victory was determined by what was going on in my life, and I continuously struggled with letting my emotions control my choices. Since separating from my wife, my emotions were a mess. So on that Sunday night I got high and just watched television. When I got tired, I went to bed.

When I woke up, I immediately knew something was different. There was a lightness that is hard to explain. I didn't understand it as I got ready for work. All I can say is that I was different.

When I got to work, I was able to follow the procedures to open the business, but it was strange. My perception of life had changed. "All things had become new" (2 Cor. 5:17). I don't know how to explain it. I was different. Many things happened that week that gave me pause, wondering what had happened to me. The most obvious thing I noticed was that I had absolutely no interest in smoking marijuana. None!

Jesus had reached into my soul and brought about true and complete healing. How do I know it was a complete healing? Because ever since that Sunday night, *decades ago,* I have never been tempted to get high. Not once. I have had occasions to be around it, when people were all but blowing smoke in my face. But it was as if I had never used it, as if it had never been in my life to begin with. The adversary knows what happened, and he has never tried to tempt me again with it. How Jesus goes about bringing a healing like that is beyond me. But I'm living proof that He can do it.

It seems that the healing of my desire for getting high had other ramifications for my life. I really didn't understand myself and the things I started doing, and that was out of character for me. God began sending me opportunities to be used by Him. A lady with three small kids showed up at work. I found out that she was in need, and I gave her some money and helped her secure housing. I lent my car to another lady, who had recently returned to church after about twenty years, so that she could get her kids to school and find a job. God performed a miracle, using me to find this family an apartment when supposedly there was none available.

I probably get no greater satisfaction from anything I do more than from, despite my selfish heart, giving to others and asking nothing in return. Helping these people and others brought a joy I had never experienced before. I was getting a glimpse of what Christianity is all about. James 1:27 says, "Pure religion … is this: to visit orphans and widows in their trouble." I was learning some fundamental truths about what following Jesus is all about.

I continued marveling about the changes that Jesus had brought to my life. I was so different. It was like my personality was vanilla ice cream. After a while some nuts started to appear, then some chocolate chips, then some mint. I was a different person. These blessings came to me probably because of my secular background, which left me with many wounds and a very hard heart. If Jesus can soften my heart, He can soften anyone's.

Yet another lesson came out of the experience of my marriage breaking up. By moving into an apartment, I was setting up a second household, and that increased my expenses. Though both my wife and I had been working, we were still living paycheck to paycheck. We had little savings. As time went by, I was amazed at how God was covering expenses for both households. *It seemed the more money I gave away, the more I had.* I wasn't getting rich, but everything was covered. "The generous soul will be made rich, and he who waters will also be watered himself" (see Prov. 11:25). This promise doesn't necessarily guarantee financial success, but it emphasizes the richness of the soul, which is far greater than gold or silver.

Another significant event dovetailed with these changes. I had started going to a campus ministry that our church had started at Chico State. A large house had been strategically rented on a busy corner of the campus. A young lady lived there and directed several outreach programs. At one of the Bible studies, I noticed a young man I recognized from church. He had a bushy blond hairdo that looked like something from a Beach Boys song. In meeting him, I found that he had just heard about the Sabbath. He and a couple of friends were checking out the church. He didn't have much going on in his life and was barely making it. He had little of this world's goods. He would wear the same dirty white tee shirt and battered jeans every Sabbath. But he was always smiling, and he loved to talk about Jesus. He had what he called "a pocket ministry." He carried a pocketful of little Bible promise cards and he would randomly pass them out. God really blessed; he always seemed to pull out just the right promise to meet a person's need.

One Sabbath he walked up to me and flashed a promise card at me. It hit me hard. It was so pertinent. I couldn't believe it. I almost looked up toward the sky at the moment, all but expecting an angel to be over our heads. God certainly had control of the cards in his pocket. The promise spoke directly to my immediate experience. It was Malachi 4:2: "But to you who fear [reverence] My name the Sun of Righteousness shall arise with healing in His wings; And you shall go out and grow fat like stall-fed calves."

What an appropriate promise! It spoke directly to my heart. Jesus was bringing healing to my life. Further, I was spiritually growing like a calf in the stall. A calf, if fed properly, grows very rapidly following birth. So, this is what was happening to me?

That promise from Malachi signaled a change in the direction of my devotional and study times. Since I had moved into the apartment, the Holy Spirit had me focusing on Proverbs and those two volumes of the *Testimonies*. I call Proverbs the "Book of Christian Living." And I needed help in learning how to live as a Christian. The focus of my time with God changed. I found myself immersed in the Gospels and a book on Jesus' life called *The Desire of Ages* (White). I couldn't put that book down, reading it in just a few days. This set a focus for my devotional life that has lasted to this day. Over the years, many of Jesus' promises in the Gospels have become precious to me. They are what keep me going, especially in the hard times.

The promises of God are for everyone, and there is a treasure trove of these promises in the Bible. There are literally thousands to claim as our own. They cover every aspect of our lives. They are helps for daily living. They are our help in time of need. Claiming the promises will increase and mature my faith as I encounter the upward way to heaven. When the Apostle Peter said at Pentecost, "And it shall come to pass *that* whoever calls on the name of the LORD shall be saved" (Acts 2:21), we can take it to the bank. And there are many other promises to help us along the way. Again, "God stands back of every promise He has made" (White, *Christ's Object Lessons,* p. 147).

Wow! The Creator of the universe, and the one who re-creates our hearts, the one who holds up worlds, guarantees each promise. Our part is to believe what God has promised. These were hard lessons for me to learn, but by the grace of God, I was learning them!

4.

Answered Prayers!

When God's time to work in someone's life has come, absolutely nothing can stop Him. The story of Joseph, in the book of Genesis, is a prime example of God's timing. After Joseph was unjustly sold as a slave and lingered in prison for a few years, God took him from the dungeon and made him the second-most-powerful man in the world. All, perhaps, in just twenty-four hours!

God's timing is perfect. And though I certainly wasn't in Joseph's class, my time had come. Things were changing. I was changing. A whole new experience was about to open in my life, though I wouldn't comprehend the breadth of the change for quite a while.

> *Things were changing. I was changing. A whole new experience was about to open in my life, though I wouldn't comprehend the breadth of the change for quite a while.*

One night in 1983, there was a knock on my door. A new friend of mine, a young man I had met at an evangelism series, was standing, looking kind of helpless, in my doorway. He had been baptized just two months earlier.

"I was going to the elder's house," he said, with a tone of desperation in his voice that struck a chord in me, "but I couldn't find it. I've been there before, but I couldn't find it tonight. So I decided to come see if you could help me with a problem."

He came in and we sat in my living room discussing a problem he was struggling with. As a new Christian, he was susceptible to rumors and stories he was hearing about the church and had become upset; he still didn't understand that only Jesus is perfect, not His people. Little did I know that this was going to be a pivotal moment for me; this friend was the first person God sent to me for counsel. I didn't realize that God had begun the process of taking me out of the business world and giving me a new career as a licensed counselor. It's amazing how God manifests His plan for someone's life, even as He works through our selfish desires, weaknesses, and wounds, all in order to bring about what is best for us. And He does it without infringing on our freedom of choice. What a God!

It wasn't much later that Jesus' plans for me began to unfold. One day, the owner of the business I managed came to town unannounced but with an announcement. After seven years of successfully managing his business, I was told that I was going to be laid off, for at least four months. That was it. The national economy was in a downturn, which caused a recession.

So much had changed in my life that I wasn't really all that surprised. When the owner told me, I thought, Praise God! He was going to move to Chico and run the business. It wouldn't be right away, so I had the opportunity to make plans for the time I wasn't working for him.

I didn't know what I would do. But God knew, and He would eventually let me know, as well. He always has a plan. If only I could see that clearly, I would have less anxiety and more peace.

After several days of praying, He let me know in a one-of-a-kind communication. I was vacuuming my apartment one day and was talking with Jesus about what He wanted me to do. Then, for the first and only time, I heard God speak to me in an audible voice. He said, "Move down with your mother."

I was stunned and sat down to contemplate what had just happened. God spoke to me! The God who spoke to Moses in the burning bush, who spoke to young Samuel in the temple, now spoke to me, Barry Pratt! It was very clear. My prayers had been answered. Why Jesus chose to speak to me audibly—I don't know. I know only that He did! Maybe it was because He knew that I loved living in Chico and only something that direct would get my attention. But it was clear that I was to move down to the Bay Area, where I had grown up and wasn't particularly excited about returning to.

Moving back to my hometown was an interesting proposition. It brought back many memories. One day while driving down a major artery of town, I was surprised to see a very large church dominating the area. It was Seventh-day Adventist! It was surprising because for the twenty-four years that I had lived in my hometown, I must have bicycled or driven by that church hundreds of times and never noticed it. It showed me how, before I met Jesus, I lived in a different world, with different thoughts and motivations, than I did after I met Him. I see so much more with Jesus than without Him.

My mother, who was a widow for several years by now, had been stricken with a severe case of rheumatoid arthritis many years before, at the age of forty-nine. She had recently sold our family home and moved into a condominium. She was due to have surgery on one of her deformed hands. So I called to let her know about my plan to move down for four months. It is amazing how God can blend plans so that several needs can be addressed at the same time. Over about a six-week period, my mother's surgery had been postponed twice due to situations with her surgeon. It was rescheduled for the day after I arrived! Without those delays, I wouldn't have been able to help her. God can even manipulate surgery schedules to bring about His plans. After the surgery, I was able to take her to daily therapy, help with home therapy, shop, and prepare meals. My mother had already undergone two surgeries, which left her with stainless-*steel knees. She was also on some powerful medication. She definitely needed some help.

Moving in with my mother was an unknown. We didn't always have the best of relationships. I was not the best son. My selfish choices caused many problems for us. As I mentioned, my mother was a product of the Great Depression. She was the next-to-youngest in a large family and had experienced difficult times. Needing some kind of income though barely a teenager, she was allowed to leave home and join an acrobatic dance group that traveled around the Midwest. I always wondered what type of difficulties and traumas she might have faced in that circumstance. This and other situations left her prejudiced and hardened toward life and toward others. It soon became obvious to me that there were more reasons for my coming than just helping her. The reasons were huge, as I would find out in God's time. One reason that immediately occurred to me was that Jesus wanted to heal our relationship. That's His main business. He came to earth to repair not only our vertical relationship with the Father, but also our horizontal relationships with others. Learning how to love my neighbor was not easy for me. Loving my enemy was still down the road a way.

God worked things out so that my boss could sublet my apartment until I returned. My understanding of the scope of God's attention and influence in my life was expanding. He is interested in even the small details. I've come to believe that the small miracles of life are more revealing of God's interest and ability to bless my life than are the occasional large ones. Leaving Chico was not easy. Leaving friends, a beautiful area of Northern California, a secure job, and the only church I knew was very hard. But it was only for four months, right? *Only four months.* That thought is what got me through those early days.

After her surgery, my mother and I developed a routine. Make meals, do her hand therapy, watch her favorite television programs, take her to see her doctor for more therapy, shop when needed, and various other things. Yet not working was uncomfortable for me. My interior life ran at a quick pace, which generally means impatience. Trying to slow down was difficult and demanding, though it became clear to me that Jesus wanted to work in this area of my life.

Thus, I sought to make changes. In every encounter with someone, for example, I would allow them to go ahead or first, depending on the situation. When shopping, I would choose the *longest* check-out line instead of the shortest. I would park farther away from a store instead of up close. By far, the most difficult was to drive at the new speed limit of 55 mph, which had been enforced by California law. As time went by, I began seeing the benefit of slowing down. Jesus had placed me in a situation where He could work on me. He was blessing my efforts. One of the highest blessings Jesus wants to give me is peace. In John 14:27, He told His disciples, "Peace I leave with you, My peace I give to you; not as the world gives do I give to you. Let not your heart be troubled, neither let it be afraid." I continue to pursue peace to this day.

Because I was going to be in the area for only four months, I casually attended a couple of local churches for Sabbath worship. One was the large one that I had seen earlier—the largest Adventist church that I had ever attended. I was told that many people who were associated with Pacific Press, which was nearby, attended.

At one church I met a lady who needed help moving some items. I agreed to help, and when I arrived at her place, some others were already there. Things went quickly and, as I was leaving, I noticed a stack of books by the front door. I asked if she wanted me to put them in a specific place. She said I could have them. Looking at the books I realized that they were about prayer. They were by one author, Glenn Coon. I had read his classic book *ABC's of Prayer* a couple of years before. I didn't know he had written other books, and I gladly took them home. Over the next few weeks, I read every one. They changed my life. I was impressed, as never before, about the power, the importance, and the need for prayer. What a blessing that lady shared with me. These books were the foundation of my calling to prayer ministry.

Time was passing; I had two things in mind. One was going back to Chico and picking up my life where I had left off. The other thing that started mildly nagging my mind was whether my mother was going to be able to continue living on her own. My sister was about thirty minutes away, but she was a widow and had two kids of her own to take care of. I began to pray about it. As the last of the four months was approaching, I began to assess my mother's situation more closely, and how well, or not, she was handling life. She seemed to be doing fine, but it was difficult to tell just how fine because I was doing a lot for her.

> *With God I have the right to choose my way and He will continue to work in my life. But He has a plan for my life, and I wanted to live out His plan, not mine.*

Then I received a call from my boss. He was inquiring about my situation and about returning to work. This set me on a course of deep soul searching. First, I dealt with my own desire. I missed Chico terribly and all that it had meant to me for so many years. But I was learning a little about how Jesus works in my life. I really struggled with the concept of "not my will, but Yours, be done" (see Luke 22:42). The conflict in my mind increased. My boss called back a couple of days later, offering a new pay rate. It was less than what I had been making, even with a bonus attached. This gave me even more to contemplate. My desire to return was strongly pulling on my heart, even with a reduction in pay. I asked Jesus to show me clearly what He wanted me to do.

I happened to be reading a book by Morris Venden at the time. Pastor Venden was a popular writer, speaker, and evangelist for many years. I came to a section on making decisions. One sentence stuck out. It said something to the effect that *when you have a difficult decision, you will have peace if you make the correct choice.* With that in mind, I made the choice, against my desire, not to return to Chico but, instead, to continue to take care of my mother. A tremendous peace came over me. I knew I had made the right decision. Along with that peace came the realization that I would not be returning to Chico. With God I have the right to choose my way and He will continue to work in my life. But He has a plan for my life, and I wanted to live out His plan, not mine. As I look back, that decision was one of the most important decisions that I had ever made, for it sent me on a trajectory that would completely change my life.

I called my boss. He was upset, but he seemed to understand. I made a trip to Chico to put my affairs in order, then off I went on a journey whose outcome I could not have imagined. It was an emotional time for me. But I had made a choice that led to peace. I tried to keep that in mind. There was a period of mourning, for sure, as I drove and had time to think, with some satisfaction and some painful regret, about my years in Chico.

Upon moving in with my mother and getting somewhat settled in, I realized that I could qualify for unemployment benefits because of my layoff. So I visited the local employment development department (EDD) and applied. Little did I know what I was in for. The process was slow because of the large number of people out of work due to the recession. The Bay Area is much larger than Chico, and I hadn't imagined the number of unemployed people I would be encountering. There was much waiting and paperwork! As I've mentioned, I wasn't good at waiting. Sitting in the office waiting for my number to be called was difficult. This was before cell phones and computers were common. My nature was set on *wanting something and wanting it right now*. I was highly impatient. Jesus knew that and continued working on my impatience—by making me have to sit for long painful intervals in the waiting room. I had no choice. Finally, having applied and being qualified for benefits, I thought I was past the waiting and confusion of going to the office. But I soon found out that the EDD had trouble with someone who was honest.

Paperwork was required every week, to document the progress of your job search. At the end of each week, the paperwork needed to be mailed in to the EDD. My job was highly specialized at the time; not many commercial recreation businesses did what I had been doing. So it didn't take long to locate the four or five businesses that might make use of my experience. I reported each contact, as required, to the EDD and received regular benefit checks. After a few weeks, though, I had run out of legitimate businesses to inquire about work.

In my pre-Christian days, I simply would have lied on the forms and said that I was still looking for work. But I was different now. Once I met Jesus, I was determined to be honest in all things. I sent in my forms stating that I hadn't looked for work that week. I received an appointment time in the mail and had to go to the office to meet with an eligibility worker. Prayerfully, I showed up at the appointment to explain my situation and informed the worker that I was being honest. The worker seemed a little abrupt. I also told him about the lack of opportunity to find work in my field. That seemed to be enough for him; I left and continued to receive benefits. This happened two more times, causing me to have two more interviews. The last worker was a little perturbed and seemed to hint that I should be a little less forthcoming. I didn't realize that my honesty was causing her extra work. But by God's grace, the benefits kept coming.

Because of the downturn in the economy, the government started giving extensions on benefits, and that prolonged my stay in the system. A few months passed, and I was struggling with being jobless. I was not one to sit around doing nothing. Even though there was enough to do for my mother, I wanted to work, even if it was in a new field or part time. Looking in the newspaper and going to the EDD was not very satisfying. The economic situation made the job market tough. A couple of interviews were fruitless. When God closes a door, no man can open it. I was becoming more watchful for God's leading. For an impatient man, that was not easy. So I continued receiving benefits. Then an extension, then another. I was starting to climb the walls.

One day, while shopping at JCPenney with my mother, I noticed a small sign by the entrance, *Hiring for Christmas*. I found myself sitting in a small office and filling out an application while my mother shopped. This led to an interview, which led to a seasonal job offer. The supervisor apologized for not being able to match my previous pay schedule. Little did he know that my working there wasn't about the money; it was about doing something productive and being in a work environment. I started a few weeks before Christmas. Oh, what joy it was to be working, even if it was in a stockroom! My main responsibility was rearranging stock to make more room for the glut of seasonal Christmas goods. I don't think that I ever enjoyed working more than I did there. The job, of course, ended my stint of unemployment benefits.

Because of what was happing with the economy, sales were down. So just before Christmas, Penney's laid off a number of seasonal workers, including me. I received my last check and tried to enjoy the Christmas season. A few days after New Year's, a friend from Chico called about a a recreation enterprise that was going to be built. It was going to be a large miniature golf course with a video-game center—exactly my line of work. The pull of returning to Chico was revived. Forgetting God's leading in my decision to be there to help my mother, I made plans to go to Chico and check things out. With my experience, I would be a good fit for the new enterprise.

Before I left for Chico, another situation arose: I received a letter from the EDD that stated that I might qualify for a new claim for benefits. There must be some mistake, I thought. If it wasn't a mistake, that could mean that I might continue to be unemployed, and I didn't want that! The letter said that if I had earned $1200 since my last claim ended, which happened when I worked for JCPenney, then I would be eligible. Fortunately, I had kept my last pay stub. I was relieved to find that I had earned only $1120 during my time at Penney's. To me, that meant I couldn't qualify for another claim and a job must be in my future! I had no evidence that a job was imminent except my desire for what *I wanted*. In other words, I didn't see a sign that I should stay in the Bay Area. Ah, the struggles when the self wants its own way.

So I went to Chico to check out the potential opportunity. I was enthused because the opportunity seemed to be something in which my experience would be helpful. As I drove, I spent a great deal of time in prayer, asking Jesus to make things clear. Really though, my desire was to return to Chico. I wasn't being honest with myself in asking for God's will. Upon further investigation, I found out two things. First, it was going to be a family-run business. Though this didn't necessarily mean that I couldn't be hired, it meant that a management position wasn't probable. Second, there were multiple investors in the project, and it was many months away from completion. A few months later I learned that the project had fallen apart and the investors had lost their money. While in Chico I called my mother, to check in. She told me JCPenney had called and wanted me to get in touch. They offered me a week's worth of work doing end-of-the-year inventory. I decided to take the work and hurriedly returned to the Bay Area.

I thought that Jesus had shut the door on returning to Chico. Really, the door had never been open. Such is the deception of selfishness. I talked myself into believing God had presented an opportunity. When I returned home, I worked the week doing inventory and was thankful for it. A couple of weeks later, I received another letter from the EDD. It had an appointment attached to it for another office visit. Now what? The next week I went to the appointment. While waiting in the outer office, I prayed for wisdom and understanding. When it was my turn, I sat down at the worker's desk. I showed her the previous letter and pointed out that I didn't qualify. She looked at my case and said that yes; I did, in fact, qualify!

As it turned out, the week of inventory work put me over the qualifying amount of $1,200. I had earned $140 doing the inventory work, raising my total to $1,260. I was dumbfounded. The worker looked at me and said, "That's a miracle." Adding what I made doing the inventory put me $60 over the minimum of $1,200. I qualified. Her statement came across her desk like a megaphone that rang in my ears. The Holy Spirit spoke; no, He yelled, at me in order to make a deep impression. He knew that when the shock wore off, I would have trouble accepting the answer to my prayer for understanding. I needed to stay here, be unemployed, and not go back to Chico.

> *Thinking back over the previous few weeks, I realized that the hand of God had orchestrated a number of incidents, with perfect timing, to bring about what He wanted for me.*

After a couple of days, and more prayer, I decided that I needed to accept the situation as God's will. With that decision, I had some peace. So what was I to do? Thinking back over the previous few weeks, I realized that the hand of God had orchestrated a number of incidents, with perfect timing, to bring about what He wanted for me. I was stunned as it became clear how involved He was in my life. He knows even the inner working of the EDD and how to bring about the results He wanted! As things continued to become clear, I kept on thinking about what the woman in the office uttered before. *That's a miracle!* It was.

But this was only the beginning.

5.

The Bicycle

Here I was, possibly facing at least nine more months of unemployment benefits. I continued looking for work. But because Jesus
had demonstrated, profoundly, that for His purposes, He wanted
me out of work—I had some peace with my situation. Even though I didn't
have a job, it didn't mean that I wouldn't be working, however. And He
would be working—in me. In God's wisdom, there was work for me that
was different from putting in an eight-to-five. I continued my development as a servant by taking care of my mother. And I learned lessons that
only God could have taught me.

My mother got up every morning at ten o'clock sharp. God started
waking me up at six o'clock every morning. I would instantly be wide
awake, which wasn't natural for me. This was a small miracle in itself. But
Jesus had a plan and a purpose. He wanted to spend time with me. Yes,
the Creator and Sustainer of the universe wanted to spend time with me!
He wanted to teach me the richest lesson that a Christian can learn—the
devotional life, that is, spending time in His presence. Communicating
with Him. Sharing what was on my heart. Learning to understand how He
speaks to me. Up until then, I didn't have much of a devotional life. For
some reason, prayer had always been important to me, but it was never
formalized into a specific devotional time. The Glenn Coon books had
increased my knowledge about the power of prayer and claiming Bible
promises. Now Jesus wanted me to learn a different facet of prayer. A
deeper, more intimate form of prayer. Prayer is an entering into the presence of God. The heavenly sanctuary is the very center, the heartbeat,
of the universe, because Jesus is there. It is praising, singing, expressing
adoration and joy, simply because you are in His presence. Being in His
presence is safe, comforting, healing, sanctifying, and beautiful.

King David was one of the greats of the Bible, one whom God called
"a man after His own heart" (see 1 Sam. 13:14). He's someone to pay
attention to, whether he was doing good or bad. In Psalm 27, David says
this about being in God's presence:

49

"One *thing* I have desired of the LORD, that will I seek: That I may dwell in the house of the Lord all the days of my life. To behold the beauty [delightfulness] of the Lord, and to inquire in His temple" (verse 4).

The *one* thing, the *main* thing, that the great King David desired was to be in God's temple. Why? What for? To behold the delightful character of God. To bask in His glory, His grace, His love. Sanctification comes by being in God's presence. Now we see in a mirror, dimly, but I yearn for the time when we will see Him face to face, and be able to sit physically in His presence! (See 1 Cor. 13:12.) Come, Lord Jesus!

How do I come into God's presence, right now, this very hour? Through prayer. And as with all things, it's because of Jesus that I can come into the heavenly sanctuary at any time, through prayer. The writer of Hebrews tells us that because of what Jesus did while on this earth, we can "come boldly [confidently] to the throne of grace, that we may obtain mercy and find grace to help in time of need" (Heb. 4:16). Because of Jesus, the way to the heavenly sanctuary is open to us through prayer.

I knew nothing of these things when Jesus started waking me up to teach me about the devotional life. Learning to communicate with Jesus is something that I have been pursuing for more than thirty years now. Those things that are important to me is what Jesus wants to hear about. I can talk to Him like a trusted friend. It was here, in my mother's condominium, that it all began for me. Talking to the Father in Jesus' name, contemplating from the Scripture Jesus' earthly life, is an ever-growing revelation.

The result that God is looking for is summarized in 2 Corinthians 3:18, which in essence says, *By beholding Jesus we become changed into His image.* This is an unchangeable spiritual law. If we behold Jesus, we will be changed into His image. That's what I want! The other side of the coin is also an unchangeable law: If I behold the simulated crime and sex in the media or the vain philosophies of the world, I will be changed into that image. Beholding Jesus in our devotional life is the touchstone for our development as Christians.

One morning, as I knelt for prayer, a strange thing happened. I didn't know it, but I was about to go on a journey that would take me through a series of crazy, humbling, and embarrassing wild rides. As I began praying, the image of a bicycle came crystal clear to my mind. *A bicycle?* Along with this image, a truly hideous feeling accompanied it. It was the worst feeling I have ever experienced. There wasn't any pain, just a deep ugliness. I didn't know what to do. What was going on? It was devastating!

There was no answer, and my devotional time was ruined for that day. And every devotional for at least a week was disrupted. I was pleading for an answer. Every morning, first thing as I began to pray, the same image and overwhelming feeling was present. I agonized with God for hours during that week. What is this all about? What are you trying to tell me?

Finally, Jesus answered. As I knelt in prayer, He gave me understanding. It wasn't a vision or anything like that; it was more like my mind being opened to understand. Jesus revealed that the bicycle was from my past. I knew, in an instant, the circumstances and meaning of the bicycle. In one of my many ethically-challenged choices years before—I had stolen it.

> *As I began praying, the image of a bicycle came crystal clear to my mind. A bicycle? Along with this image, a truly hideous feeling accompanied it. It was the worst feeling I have ever experienced.*

What happened was this. I was going to be leaving for Chico in two days, to enter the university. I had been out drinking with friends until early morning. I had made a deal with a friend to trade a ten-speed bicycle for a large grocery bag of home-grown marijuana. I would be set for the school year. Inebriated, I set out to find a nice bicycle to steal. I found myself in front of the home of a friend. I knew the family well. They had five kids. I knew they had several bicycles, which would be in front of their house. I rationalized in my drunken state that, because the father was a dentist, it wouldn't be a burden for them to replace the bicycle. So I took it. The following day I traded it as planned, and I was off to Chico.

Now that I knew what the Lord was doing within me, I understood the source of my inner turmoil. But what was I to do with this knowledge? And what did the dreadful feelings represent? I was relieved yet still questioning. Relieved because I finally understood about the bicycle, but still questioning what it all meant. What also remained was the question of the terrible feelings that accompanied the image of the bike. In a subsequent devotional time, Jesus used some Scripture to show me what was at the root of those dreadful feelings.

In Genesis 3, we have the fall of Adam and Eve in the Garden of Eden. The last verse of chapter 2 addresses Adam and Eve's condition *before* the fall, "And they were both naked, the man and his wife, *and were not ashamed*" (emphasis added). In the pristine atmosphere of a perfect world, the couple was naked and felt no shame. Moving forward to chapter 3, we see the terrible picture of the first result of the fall. In verse 7, after the fatal decision was made to disobey God, they experienced a new reality and "they knew that they *were* naked; and they sewed fig leaves together and made themselves coverings." The implication is that before the fall, the couple were unashamed of their nakedness; after the fall, in a new reality, their nakedness was shameful to them, and they tried to hide that shame by covering themselves with leaves. As I digested this information, I was deeply impressed that the feelings I was consumed with were a manifestation of shame—a large dose of it. I decided to find out what Jesus had in mind for me concerning this newly found issue.

So I continued to pray. Almost immediately I knew what I had to do. It became obvious to me that I had to make things right concerning the bicycle. Jesus wanted me to pay back what I had taken. Yikes! How was I going to do that? About thirteen years had passed. How was I to find the person I had stolen the bicycle from? The thought of admitting to someone what I had done was humiliating, and it brought much fear. Could I get myself to do it?

I became immobilized from dread. I would find anything to do except what I knew I needed to do. This increased my unease until, anxiously, I moved forward. I started by looking in the local phone book, and it took me about two minutes to find the family's address. It was the same address they'd always had. Jesus had made it easy for me. To figure out what to do next wasn't easy, though. Was I just to show up at their door and talk to whoever answered? I wasn't sure if any of the kids I'd known still lived there. I decided to call first and find out if any of them were still in the home.

I don't think I have ever made a more difficult call in my life, but I'm pretty sure Jesus arranged everything ahead of time. The call went well. One of the sisters I had gone to school with answered. I identified myself and made some small talk. Then I told her I wanted to come by and talk with her younger brother. It was his bicycle. She asked me to come over that afternoon and he would be there. Wow! As easy as that! I immediately got on my knees to pray. I admitted to Jesus that I was scared to death. What an embarrassing situation. I decided that I would offer him $100 for the bicycle. I never imagined a situation like this as a possibility. But obviously Jesus knew, and He saw what could come out of the situation to bless them and me. It never ceases to amaze how Jesus can take events from any time in my life and use them for His glory and my growth!

That afternoon, I anxiously drove over to their house. I had a lot of inner turmoil and an upset stomach. I was sweating bullets. I didn't know who would be there or what I would say or how they would react. The adversary was oppressing me with much fear and anxiety. I prayed that Jesus would send the Holy Spirit ahead of me to arrange what He wanted to happen. I also prayed for Him to give me the words to say. I was a mess, trembling, fearful, as I came to the door. The same sister I had talked with on the phone, answered the door. She was three grades behind me, so I didn't know her as well as her older brother and sister. She invited me in and said her brother was due home any minute. While we waited, I told her I was a Christian. She replied that she was a Baptist, and that surprised me because, when I knew them before, they were Roman Catholic. She told me the family was split over religion. The parents and one of the older siblings were still Catholic; she and two other children had become Protestant. The brother I was going to talk with was the only one in the family who wasn't committed to any religion.

He promptly arrived. I was surprised at how much he had grown to look like his older brother. I didn't know what to say. He started the conversation by saying that he was coming from an auto mechanic because of a problem with his car. He was lamenting that the repair estimate was more than he could afford. We were sitting around a table and I slowly worked around to the reason I was there. I told them a shortened story about my encounters with seeing the bicycle in my prayers. Then I just told them about stealing his bicycle. He seemed a little amused and his sister's mouth dropped open. Being a Christian, she seemed to understand what was happening. I told him Jesus wanted me to pay him back, and I offered the $100 in cash, five twenty-dollar bills, that I had in my pocket.

He gladly took the money and told me there was no grudge. Before I knew it, I was saying, "Do you see how Jesus provided for your car repair?"

That had an impact on him; his sister had a big smile on her face. We talked a little longer and then I left. I was both washed out and elated as I got back into my car. I never had experienced a situation like that before. It was heavy. I didn't know it then, but I was going to become well acquainted with this kind of experience.

Almost immediately, I was convicted about other situations Jesus wanted me to clean up. In my late teens and early twenties, shoplifting and petty theft was how I got through life. With those illicit activities, I always had money to do what *I wanted*; that is, I always had gas in my car, and could buy whatever alcohol or drugs I thought I needed. I was morally challenged in those days. Selfishness overruled honesty.

In short, I had a series of experiences, as with the bicycle. I didn't have images during my devotionals as I did with the bicycle, but God made things very clear. When I would shop in town, the Holy Spirit would tap me on the shoulder and say, *Do you remember what you took from that store?* This happened about six or seven times. It got to the point where I didn't want to shop in my own town.

When those ugly feelings of shame would come up, I realized the Holy Spirit was calling. I would spend time in prayer asking what Jesus wanted me to do. Then I would anxiously go to the store and ask for the owner or manager. I can't describe the overwhelming fear, along with profuse perspiration and dry mouth. Sometimes I would have to wait ten to fifteen minutes for the clerk to finish with a customer before I could talk with him or her. What an ordeal! How humiliating! When I would finally get to talk to someone, usually the owner, I would identify myself and tell them why I was there. I would tell them that many years earlier I had stolen items from their store (sunglasses, candy, bath items, clothes, etc.). And that Jesus had told me to come in and make restitution.

The reactions were remarkable. The impact was Spirit led. Most were dumbfounded and didn't know what to say. All were kind as they regained their footing. I'm sure they hadn't encountered this type of situation before. I would give them some money, which I had prayerfully decided on. Every person, without exception, thanked me for my honesty. As I left the store, a tremendous burden would lighten, like taking off a backpack full of rocks. And what a witness to the power of the gospel these encounters must have been!

In one incident, the Spirit made it clear that I was to talk only to the owner of the store. When I talked to the clerk, he told me that at the time of my shoplifting, someone else owned the business. I asked if he knew where I could find the previous owner. In our small town, store owners knew one another, and I was directed to another business the previous owner had started. When I located that business, I found that I needed to go to another store, for there I would find the original owner of the first store. So in the end, I found the owner twice removed from where I had started. He was astonished with my story and my commitment to finding him after all those years. As I was driving home, I was overwhelmed by a glimpse of the power of God working in my life. He even knew the history and sequence of the owner of these stores; and He knew how to get me where I needed to go. I can trust a God like that!

The last store I visited wasn't in the downtown; it was a large supermarket on the outskirts of town on a busy thoroughfare. There had been times in the past when I was living on next to no money. The only way I survived was by shoplifting food and getting an occasional free burger from a friend who worked at a fast-food restaurant. I had gone to this supermarket several times and stolen meat. I was very good at stuffing steaks into my pants. I would buy a can of soup or some other cheap item to be "legitimate" at the checkout.

Because of my previous experience with other stores, I wasn't quite as anxious as before. I asked for the manager; an East Indian man wearing a Sikh headdress approached me. When I expressed to him that I was a Christian and that God had told me to reimburse the store for what I had taken, his eyes became like saucers. He put his hands together and slightly bowed to me. He was obviously overwhelmed by the circumstances. It wasn't me, but I think the idea of someone making such a gesture, that really impressed him.

There were a couple of other large enterprises that came to mind but were no longer in business. I did a little research and found their parent companies and sent them letters with some money. This was easier, by a long shot, than going to the stores

Also, three incidents from when I was in college came back to my mind. These are things I had done to enhance grades.

The first was a situation where I didn't do anything illegal, but I benefited from a classmate's doings. We were taking an art history class together and, as usual, I wasn't doing very well. My friend was flunking the class. One weekend he was partying at a hotel. On the way out, he stole a four-foot hand-carved wooden statuette from the entrance. A couple of days later, he asked me if I would go with him to our art professor's office and support him, as he would offer the professor the statuette for a passing grade. The professor, a tall, portly man who looked as if he had stayed too long at the bar at the art openings he would tell the class about, asked no questions and readily agreed to the trade. Though I didn't say anything, the professor must have assumed I was part of the deal; my D in the class was upped to a B. My friend went from an F to a C. (At the time, my choice of "friends" was based on a sandy foundation—obviously.)

The second incident happened at Chico State. I took an English class called Film as Literature. We studied some of the great movies of the past and the way movies were made. There was only one assignment at the end of the semester, which constituted the grade. As usual, I was behind and wasn't going to get the assignment finished. So I paid a friend to write the paper for me. I knew he was a good writer; I got an A in the class.

The third incident was such that only the adversary could have set up the circumstances and timing. At this point, I was completely naïve about the reality of the great controversy. The way the situation played out as it did, absolutely amazes me to this day.

I was taking a sociology class and, of course, wasn't doing too well. A single paper was required at the end of the semester, and it constituted the whole grade; I didn't complete it. I went to the professor to ask for more time. When I approached his door, I noticed that it was wide open. I stuck my head into his office and found it empty. I walked in and wondered if I should wait for him. While I was deciding, my eye fell on his desk, which was completely clean—except for a small black book wide open and a pen next to it. I walked over to his desk; it was his grade book! Next to it was the pen he used to enter grades.

It dawned on me what could occur. I began to sweat and wondered if I could find my class in the book. I quickly went back to the door and looked both ways down the corridors. No one in sight. I went back to his desk, hoping to find the right class. I was trembling so much that I was reluctant to pick up the little book. But I didn't have to. Unbelievably, it was open to my class! *How could this be?* I looked down the list and found my name. It stuck out because there were completed grades before and after my name, but no grade by mine. There it was! A chance to pass the class. I briefly wondered if I could enter a B, which would blend in with the other grades. My hand was shaky, but I felt good about the letter I entered. I immediately exited the office and stopped around the corner to take several deep breaths to calm down. The possibility of that event happening as it did are astronomical. The situation, timing, and opportunity are mind boggling.

Then years later, amid this time of my seeking to amend for my past ways, I ended up writing letters to the schools and explaining that, as a Christian, I was confessing these deeds and leaving the response to them. I didn't hear back from either of the schools. I always wondered about the effect the letters had on the people who read them, and if they were spread around the administration. We never know the extent of an act we do in accordance with the Holy Spirit's leading.

What were the reasons God had for all of these events? Why would He put this sequence of trials in my life and bring to mind events of my past?

One reason is that He loves me and wants the best for me—to bring healing to my sin-sick soul and develop my character. At that time, He had gotten hold of me in a deeper way through get-

> *Then I realized that the main reason for these events was to see if I would be obedient.*

ting me to have a regular devotional life. That gave Jesus opportunity for richer and deeper communication between us. All I had to do was give Him that opportunity. It was my choice.

I realized that it wasn't about paying back the money. I didn't pay back four-fold as Zacchaeus did (see Luke 19:8). That was not the point. Nor was it about making things right with people and institutions for things I had done. No doubt, all of these things had some importance in cleaning up my heart; Jesus never wastes an opportunity. As I prayed, I asked what Jesus wanted me to learn from the whole of these events. Then I realized that the main reason for these events was to see if I would be obedient. Obedient to doing what He called me to do—no matter the humiliation, embarrassment, and shame. Obedience is important to God. The disobedience of the adversary led to the mess we are in. But most important to God is that *disobedience led to the death of His Son.*

These might seem like small things, especially in the big picture of the fall of humanity, but for God nothing is small, and He knew that I needed to do these things for me, for my own good.

I was learning lessons, lots of them, though yes, more were to come.

6.

New Directions

S ince it seemed that God had closed the door on a return to my beloved Chico, I decided to remain in the Bay Area. I started looking for a new church home. Having been a member of only one church, and not being a natural social mixer, I had a difficult time finding one. The Bay Area offered a hefty number of churches within a thirty-minute drive. So I started prayerfully attending a number of churches on a somewhat rotating basis. As time went by, I didn't feel drawn to a particular church. I continued to pray and visit around.

During this time, the waiting period for my divorce ended. I received an official-looking manila envelope in the mail with the final papers to sign. Before leaving Chico, I went to our house and I appealed one last time to my wife to resume the marriage. I told her, with all that God had changed in me over the last few months, we could have a better marriage than ever. But she wasn't interested, saying that she had moved on—with both a new man and a new job. Her words hurt a bit, but I thought her new situation was confirmation that I was to move forward in my journey.

We had gone to an attorney friend from church who was willing to help us with the paperwork—just as long as there was no fighting over terms. We worked out a fair, equitable settlement of our very modest resources. The attorney told me that, since there was no argument, only one of us needed to sign the final papers. I decided not to sign, a statement of not wanting the divorce. The papers went through anyway, and I was now, for the first time in eight years, a single man.

A few confusing things happened at some of the churches I visited, and that bothered me. Occasionally, if I would talk with someone after church, they would end up dumping their problems on me. I would think, Why are they telling me these things? Why don't they talk to the pastor or elder? They must have friends they can talk with. But no matter what I did—go on a group nature walk, a potluck supper, a Bible study, a social activity—someone would approach me. *What was going on?* I didn't know what to say, so I would find myself sharing some of my recent experiences.

It was uncomfortable for me, but often these people would say that I had helped them. I wondered what I said. It seemed this was God's way of moving me toward the new career that He had in mind for me. I was, essentially, giving counsel—but didn't know it. The Holy Spirit was using my words. What I didn't know at the time is that it can be easier for a person to tell a stranger, rather than a friend or pastor, about some difficulty they are facing. Perhaps that's why they came to me?

Jesus taught me something during this time of uncertainty. I hadn't really thought about what being single in the church meant. A few of what I now call "divine appointments," were with single women. When a simple conversation turned toward something deeper, I would cringe and feel awkward. Why is she telling me these things? I was very unsure in these situations. A few times, I was invited to someone's house after church for a potluck or some other social event. As a newly single person, I was rusty in social situations. I met a lady at one of these events and we had some good conversation. We talked on the phone a couple of times after that. A few Sabbaths later she asked me to come to her home following the potluck. After some sharing and questions about my move to the Bay Area, she started opening up about her divorce. I wasn't sure what to do. So I shared some superficial things about my divorce with her. The emotional floodgates opened; her tears flowed. I tried to calm her down, with little success. What should I do? I waited for her to calm down. I felt out of my league. I thought, Lord, why am I getting into these situations? We talked a while longer, had prayer, and I left. So what did Jesus teach me? He helped me learn that you can't date and counsel the same person!!

This situation turned out to be a template for me to follow. My senses were operating whenever I met a lady. What was happening? Was this a social encounter, or another one of those situations where I felt so inadequate? At one church, I met a married lady who had graduated from San Jose State University with a degree in psychology, and when I found out that she was a newly licensed marriage and family counselor, I related to her some of the situations which had happened over the last year or so. I asked her what she thought. I didn't like her response. She ignored my question and strongly encouraged me to go back to school and become a counselor. She said that there was great need for counselors in the Adventist church. Now going back to school was the absolute *last* thing on my mind! In fact, it had *never* crossed my mind. I didn't like school. I just wanted Jesus to teach me what He wanted me to know in order to serve Him.

A few months later, I attended an Adventist Single Ministries International Conference, at Pacific Union College, which was nearby. There were over five hundred attendees from all over the world. I really didn't know what to expect. There were single people, widowed people, divorced people—people from many parts of the world. It didn't take long to realize there were a lot of hurting people there, too. Some were lonely, some in various stages of grief, and some bitter from the wounds of divorce.

There were many choices to make during those five days. There was a plethora of worship opportunities, seminars, workshops, and social events, along with great food. The dormitory accommodations were adequate, and my bunkmate, agreeable. It was a busy time if you wanted it to be. Back then, I was one to attend as many activities as I could. There was much to choose from. Trying to keep up with everything was impossible. So I took the brochure and prayerfully chose an agenda after the first day.

As it turned out, Jesus answered my prayer and led me to several impactful meetings and events. The main speakers were licensed Christian counselors. I went to all of their seminars, not realizing they were part of the process of Jesus drawing me to a new career and giving me tools to further my own healing.

One of the areas of focus was the various issues surrounding divorce. The speaker shared tools for healing from the devastation of being torn apart after being "joined" together as "one flesh" (see Mark 10: 6–9). Torn flesh hurts. As I listened to questions and to conversations in social interactions, I could tell there were many angry people, with torn flesh. When hurt, a natural human reaction is to cover up the pain with anger. Anger gives a false sense of control because the real problem is being out of control. There is no deeper wound than a divorce because it rarely comes with closure.

I wondered, though, why I felt so little residual anger from my recent divorce. One of the speakers answered my question when he shared the topic of forgiveness as the path to healing after divorce. The speaker pointed out that forgiveness benefits the *forgiver,* not the one forgiven. This is difficult to see when you're hurting. It is a deception to believe that holding resentment hurts the other person. It hurts only the one not forgiving. I once heard someone say, "When you refuse to forgive, you're in effect handcuffing yourself to the person who offended you." Fortunately, my former wife and I had forgiven each other during the separation. We had admitted our individual failures and misdeeds that had led to the divorce. I had been convicted about my failures in my overwhelming encounters with the *Testimonies*. I realized that I needed to ask for her forgiveness, to confess! This had opened the way for her to ask for forgiveness, also. Forgiveness is one of God's greatest healing gifts, if not the greatest, for us.

Forgiveness is the center of the gospel. It stands to reason, then, that forgiveness would be central to healing the wounds of divorce since marriage is a picture of our relationship with Jesus. My problem wasn't anger, but a deep sense of failure and of letting God

> *Forgiveness is one of God's greatest healing gifts, if not the greatest, for us.*

down, an attitude that led me to want to get remarried as soon as possible because I wanted to honor God by being a good husband. It wasn't a rational desire at the time. Not being honest with myself, I wasn't able to see the fallacy of that desire because of my own need of healing. Like any other divorced person, I needed time to heal, to move on, and avoid bringing baggage into the next relationship.

When one of the speakers strongly encouraged us to let at least three years pass before getting into a serious relationship, so that healing could occur, I fully rejected that recommendation. He said that, over time, three issues needed to be addressed, to facilitate healing and preparedness for a future relationship.

The first was the divorced person's need to learn who they have become during the years of marriage. How did the relationship change them?

The second was the need to figure out and accept what their part was in the failure of the marriage. A person needs to do an honest inventory of their weaknesses and choices.

The third was dealing honestly with resentments. This can be the most difficult of the three.

The speaker stressed that if these three issues weren't addressed, the divorced person, not fully healed, was likely to take those wounds and weaknesses into their next marriage.

Though I had rejected the speaker's three-year recommendation, God didn't. I had very little social interaction in the ensuing years. After all, you can't date and counsel the same person! God used this principle to minimize my social life. And it worked! After a year, I had to admit to myself that I was healing and changing. After a second year, I began thinking that maybe the speaker had been on to something. As a third year passed, it became clear that he had real wisdom. Most of my time was spent in taking care of my mother's needs, working out at the gym, and learning more about Jesus. A verse took on a clearer meaning to me during this time. "But seek first the kingdom of God and His righteousness, and all these things shall be added to you" (Matt. 6:33). This has been a guiding principle for me. God has a plan for me and, if I put Him first in all things, He will bring into my life, and at the proper time, the things I need. It was more than four years before Jesus sent a young lady into my life. As the song goes, "Our God is an awesome God."

It still remained for me to settle into a church. I continued to pray and "church shop." Either I didn't seem to fit in at the churches, or little was happening to draw me. It's hard to explain why, but I just didn't feel comfortable in any particular congregation. I finally decided to try the Sunnyvale church, which seemed to have some things happening both spiritually and socially. Though I didn't move my membership, I started attending regularly and getting involved. I was drawn there because they offered many activities for members. I participated in as many as I could amid the responsibilities with my mother.

One of the first major events was a multi-night Revelation Seminar with the conference evangelist. It was a traditional evangelistic outreach for the Adventist church at that time. I attended as many nights as I could. I liked to pray during the meetings for the outpouring of the Holy Spirit on the evangelist and the participants. During the meetings I met a lady who was quite excited about what she was hearing. We would talk occasionally after the meetings. It was thrilling to talk with someone who was so obviously drawn by the Holy Spirit.

At the end of the meetings, she was baptized. I have never seen someone glow as she did after the baptism. She was walking six inches off the ground. We became friends. I felt different around her. There were no awkward feelings, no emotionality, no tears, and no drama. Just a friend. When someone meets Jesus and has a real conversion experience, Jesus wants to begin using that person as soon as possible. Her spiritual gifts started being revealed, one being the gift of hospitality. She began having people over to her apartment. As we got to know each other, she asked me to lead a Bible study group once a week. Later, she asked me to do a Revelation Seminar in her home. I agreed to both, and that began many years of my leading group Bible studies. She and I remain friends to this day.

A second event while I was attending Sunnyvale made my heart jump for joy when I heard about it. Glenn Coon had been invited to give his *ABC's of Prayer* seminar. What a spiritual high that week, listening to this humble man of God tell story after story about God's faithfulness in answering prayer. Of course, his focus was on the simple idea of claiming the promises of God. His ideas about claiming promises are based on the words of Jesus.

1. Ask — "Ask, and it will be given to you; seek, and you will find; knock, and it will be opened to you. For everyone who asks receives, and who that seeks finds; and to him who knocks it will be opened" (Matt. 7:7, 8).
2. Believe — "Therefore I say to you, whatever things you ask when you pray, believe that you receive *them*, and you will have *them*" (Mark 11:24).
3. Claim — "Father, I thank You that You have heard me" (John 11:41).

Number three is the prayer of reception. In this passage, Jesus thanks His Father for hearing His prayer, even *before* it is answered. *This is the key to receiving answered prayer.* It is a mixing of faith with the prayer as you claim the promise. Faith says, even before I see the answer, I thank You for giving me the answer. It takes faith to believe without seeing. The book *Education* says, "Prayer and faith are closely allied, and they need to be studied together. In the prayer of faith there is a divine science; it is a science that everyone who would make his lifework a success *must* understand" (White, p. 257, emphasis added).

> *Faith says, even before I see the answer, I thank You for giving me the answer.*

I am eternally grateful that God has revealed this simple but powerful process. It isn't a "formula prayer," as some have called it. We don't have to say some magic words in a certain order to spur God to answer. No! That's not how it works; that belief leads to a distorted view of God. He wants to answer our prayers. He wants to bless us. He has a strong desire to fulfill our needs. But it must be in His time, and in His way. He knows what is best. I fully admit I don't know how claiming promises works. But it does! (As you will see as the story continues.)

I was enjoying the fellowship and programs this church offered but, while praying, I felt no inclination to move my membership there. So I continued praying and occasionally visiting surrounding churches, wondering why nothing was becoming clear on this issue. I was beginning to realize something about myself and my walk with Jesus. As much as I didn't want to admit it, when things were not happening that *I wanted* or in the way *I thought they should,* I was usually getting in Jesus' way or was not being patient for His timing. I just had to wait on Him. I was still learning how to surrender my life to Jesus and trust in His timing. As I learned, by experience, that Jesus can be trusted in all circumstances, peace became a larger part of my life. So I continued to pray and patiently look for His leading. I continued enjoying the Sunnyvale church.

Once again, when God's time has come, nothing, absolutely nothing, can stop what He wants to happen. All the events are lined up, all the circumstances are brought together, all the players are present, and His timing is perfect. One day, I was taking my mother to an appointment. It took us into an area that I was unfamiliar with. As we were driving, I noticed a little church that I had never seen before and didn't know it existed. I wondered why, after about a year of searching for a church, I hadn't heard about this one. God's perfect timing was in play. The sign read *Mountain View Japanese Seventh-day Adventist Church* and had some Japanese characters underneath. The church was like a magnet as we drove by. I decided there and then to visit it the next Sabbath. God never ceases to surprise, and He made sure I understood His leading when His time came.

The next Sabbath, I showed up at the church. It was beautiful, with a Japanese garden and pond surrounding the bridge that connected the church and the Fellowship Hall. I found the Asian architectural influence appealing. I was learning again about God's timing, how He works in my life. When I pray and *wait* for God's plan to open up, He makes sure I don't miss it. I entered the foyer and received a warm greeting and invitation to sign the guest book. I think I was there about a minute and I knew that this was the church I was to attend. This was it! There was an immediate peace, a *comfortableness* hard to explain. I just knew. I felt as if I belonged there.

From a human standpoint, if there were a church less appropriate for me—this was it. But God had a plan. And He made it quite clear that this was the answer to my prayers and patience. God's timing is *always* perfect. It is usually my impatience and lack of faith that makes my life more difficult than it could be. But to have this church be the answer to my many prayers was amazing. Humanly speaking, it was madness. But I'm sure, to God it made perfect sense. It is only by faith that I could move forward when God revealed His plan, especially when it was so different from what was humanly expected. "For we walk by faith, not by sight" (2 Cor. 5:7).

So, the church didn't know who had just walked in their door. They didn't know me; I didn't know them. But we were to get to know each other over the next four years. Yes, four years! Because of God's plan, my four-month stay with my mother turned, ultimately, into a little more than five years! I had accepted that my time in my beloved Chico was now history. But God was moving, and I was sure as I could be that this church was a direct answer to prayer. Previously, I had made a choice not to return to work in Chico. That decision was a turning point that sent my life off in a new trajectory. Joining this church was another turning point that would send me in new directions in several areas of my life. Sometimes, God leads in strange and mysterious ways.

The church accepted me readily. But I stuck out, big time. Here was a guy who, at 6' 4," with a trimmed reddish-brown beard and short hair, was head and shoulders above almost everyone. It was a bilingual church with many first-generation Japanese. Those saints who came here from Japan were exceptionally short, making me stand out even more. Even though we couldn't communicate verbally, I could feel their warmth and friendliness. I had to learn some of their "old ways" of doing things, like bowing and having a struggle over who would go through a door first. I'm sure they exhibited a lot of grace with me.

My life was, under God's direction, moving in ways that I couldn't have imagined back then. And this was only the start.

The church provided two sermons for the bilingual congregation. After Sabbath School, everybody would gather in the main sanctuary for announcements, singing, and special music. Sometimes there would be interpretation if there were an important item that needed some discussion. Then the Japanese-speaking members would separate to a smaller room for their sermon. After church, there was always a potluck. Not just any potluck, but the best potlucks I have ever attended! The church was divided into four groups; each week one group would be responsible for preparing the dinner. Week in, week out, I was introduced to great vegetarian Asian dishes. A couple of favorites were sweet-and-sour meatballs and breaded glutton with a delightful sauce. I learned the simple pleasure of rice. Over time, my eating preferences changed for good, and that was a small part of the preparation for what God had planned for my future.

My life was, under God's direction, moving in ways that I couldn't have imagined back then. And this was only the start.

7.

Learning to Minister

Settling in, I realized that several other cultures, mostly Asian, comprised our church. At that time, Silicon Valley was erupting, bringing many Asians to America, usually to work in the computer/electronics industry or to attend nearby Stanford University. Overwhelmingly, these were young people. So there was a vibrancy in the congregation. These young people brought coworkers and fellow students from other faiths to worship. It was a melting pot and a great opportunity for the Holy Spirit to woo hearts. I interacted with many bright young people who also had great interest in the Bible. They would have their own meetings after the potluck to study some scriptural topic.

Once the congregation got to know me, they began asking me to participate in church programs; countless opportunities for service opened up. It became apparent that one reason God placed me there was for an educational experience. I grew spiritually in my years there, as I had many new opportunities. I gained experience as a Sabbath School superintendent. Back then, Sabbath School would begin with the congregation coming together to sing and hear testimonies or mission reports. Also, sometimes one of the children's divisions would be asked to recite Scripture or sing, much to the delight of the parents. Then the congregation would break up for Sabbath School to study the Bible. Though some parts of this Sabbath School have fallen by the wayside, it was an important part of the overall Sabbath worship program back then. I learned about organizing programs, preparing materials, speaking in front of a congregation, and about tactfully asking people to participate. I taught my first Sabbath School class at that church—the first of over thirty years as a Sabbath School teacher. It was here, as I learned how to teach the lesson quarterly, that I realized something about the vastness of our church. In God's wisdom, the church produced the same lesson quarterly around the world for every "nation, tribe, tongue, and people" (see Rev. 14:6). It's one of the ways God provides an opportunity for unity in our widespread last-days movement.

When asked to preach at the worship hour, I agreed, however reluctantly. Though I was barely adequate, several opportunities over the years there gave me some solid experience in the pulpit. It was helpful in learning to deal with anxiety.

I started my first prayer group, a simple intercessory prayer assemblage. We kept a shoe box of prayer requests and needs. For about three years, I would meet with four or five elderly ladies before church began. We had great fellowship and I learned about how many burdens people carry, especially about their children. This was the first of many prayer groups that I have either started or participated in. I learned that small prayer groups can change people's spiritual lives. Praying in small or large groups is one of the most important things that we, as Christians, can do. A 1967 daily devotional, *In Heavenly Places*, offers this magnificent thought: "Appeals, petitions, entreaties, between man and man, move men, and act as a part in controlling the affairs of nations. But *prayer moves heaven*" (White, emphasis added). Things, powerful things, happen when prayer is lifted up.

On occasion the pastor would ask me to help him. Since I had some flexibility with my time, I was often able to accommodate him. I didn't realize that I was learning some of the duties of a pastor. He was coming to the end of his pastoral career and had well-developed gifts. I was blessed beyond measure to observe his skills. Though sometimes there was a language barrier, watching his style of approaching people from an Asian perspective gave me an understanding that I wouldn't get anywhere else. It was a joy, and a challenge, when I would be asked to fill in for him. One time, I ended up leading a yearlong study of Daniel and Revelation for the Wednesday Prayer Meeting. I probably learned more than did the group itself.

Studying for Wednesday nights and a Sabbath School lesson every week was keeping me in the Bible, where I needed to be anyway. It was not only a blessing to prepare to share God's Word, but also a means for me to change and grow. If Christianity is anything, it is a religion of change. Spirit-led Christians, studying the Scriptures, are the most potent force for positive change in the world. Sinners become transformed by interacting with the Word. The rough becomes smooth, the proud become humble, the profligate, profitable. The Word of God is so deep and so powerful that it always gets to the heart of the matter.

"For the word of God *is* living and powerful, and sharper than any two-edged sword, piercing even to the division of soul and spirit, and of joints and marrow, and is a discerner of the thoughts and intents of the heart" (Heb. 4:12).

One time, I reluctantly accepted an invitation from some members to visit people in a nearby convalescent hospital. It was a challenge because initial social interaction doesn't come easily to me. So I paired up with another person and began visiting the patients. Almost all were bed ridden. The first couple of times I was uncomfortable and didn't like the smells. But then I noticed the positive reaction the patients had toward us and the interest we showed. You could tell that almost all had very little care shown toward them. It was sad. I look forward to the day when Jesus empties all the convalescent hospitals.

The more I went, the more comfortable I felt, until prayerfully I decided to start going on my own. The first person I visited was an angry veteran who was in bad shape. He was in his mid-thirties. I never found out exactly what his injuries were, but he'd had a progression of surgeries over the years, to try to fix his combat wounds. You could tell he wanted some social contact, but he would go into a rage easily. As we got to know each other, our conversations between his outbursts lengthened. He was angry at the government and at the military, blaming them for his injuries. He was consumed with resentment, a prime example of how holding resentments leads to emotional problems, especially anger. Nevertheless, we developed a semblance of a relationship until he left the facility. Unfortunately, he would never allow me to pray with him. I would just pray before and after we would meet.

I had one experience at the hospital that lasted for several months. One sabbath I went into a room where another church member was talking to a very old lady. She was a very distinguished lady, even in her advanced years, and even in a bathrobe. As I walked in, the lady looked at me and clearly asked, in a trembly voice, "Why did Jesus have to die on the cross?" Wow! What greater question could someone ask a Christian? I got the opportunity to answer. This was the beginning of a relationship that lasted until her death. We had an immediate connection. Her name was Mrs. Berry. We always had interplay about our names. (Berry, Barry. Get it?) In her nineties, she manifested some cognitive deterioration. I never knew how "with it" she would be when I entered her room. When she was having a good day, we had some very interesting conversations.

She had been a Christian her whole life. One day she blew my mind when she quoted all eight verses of Psalm 121. "I will lift up my eyes to the hills—from whence comes my help ... ." Over the course of our time together, she repeated this feat a few times. Amazing! The Word truly settles deeply in our memory banks. Another story she told frequently was about being a young girl in San Francisco during the great 1906 earthquake. She clearly remembered rolling back and forth across the living room floor. I never tired of her telling the story.

One Sabbath I walked into her room and found it empty. The bed was stripped, the flowers gone, the room no longer lit up by her smile. I knew it was inevitable at her age, but it was still a shock. I quickly went to the nurse's station, only to find out what I suspected—she had died. I thank God for the times we had together. I hope she will be one of my neighbors in the earth made new.

It was as if I were in a continuing education class. God kept sending me opportunities to learn and grow. One day the pastor asked me if I wanted to go to a week-long seminar at Soquel Campground, the Central California Conference (CCC) campground. The church was going to send another member, but he had to cancel. My mother felt she could make it through a week by herself, so I made sure she was stocked up, and went to the seminar. Soquel was only thirty minutes from where I was living, so I could get home quickly if I needed to.

I did not know what I was getting into. The Lay Evangelism Training Seminar (LETS) was put on once a year by the Central California Conference for one week. For me, it ended up being a turning point, an overwhelming growth spurt in my understanding of the vast array of ministries available for introducing people to Jesus. The CCC assembled many of the top soul winners in our denomination and they imparted their wisdom, insight, and experience to about sixty attendees. From the first early-morning devotion through the closing event at the end of the week, the Holy Spirit revealed Himself in a remarkable way. I had never experienced such a time.

By the third day, I had to go back to my cabin to lie down. I was overcome in a way that I had never been before. It felt as if the Spirit had taken an ax and split open my head and was pouring knowledge into my brain. To say it was overwhelming would be an understatement. The people leading the conference seemed to be filled with a Pentecostal outpouring of the Holy Spirit. The gentleman sharing the morning devotion was on fire! His focus for the week was "Behold the Man!" He spoke with power about Jesus' life. I made sure to get up early every day to make his 6:30 am meeting.

Another example of the excellence of the speakers was a couple from the General Conference. They testified that they had decided to forego having children so they would have more time to serve the Lord! Quite a decision, I must say. God must have been involved because He had blessed their ministry immensely. They were in their golden years and had introduced an untold number of people to Jesus. They talked about the many avenues of ministry they had used. From His amazing stories about witnessing to his wife's fruitful "Neighborhood Bread ministry," lifting up Jesus became more real to me.

"And I, if I am lifted up from the earth, will draw all *peoples* to myself" (John 12:32).

In a segment on lay preaching, the speaker gave several powerful insights. I had to chuckle when he went so far as to lie down on his back to demonstrate how to learn to breathe properly. He also testified about being saved as a drunken sailor who, with a beer in one hand and a cigarette in the other, started studying the Bible. This man was also an expert in door-to-door ministry. He regaled us with great stories and gave excellent pointers for encountering people at their door.

Later in the week we had two afternoons to apply some of what we learned, which included an afternoon of going door to door. I was scared to death; I had never done this before. My personality and social skills were not amenable to encountering strangers on their home turf. Though apprehensive, I went. I was assigned to go out with two African American ladies. These saints were both experienced door-to-door workers. I was open with them about my anxiety. They giggled and promised to help me. They went to the first few doors and gave their "Community Health Survey." I watched from a distance. More than two at the door can be intimidating.

Finally, it was my turn. We went to the next house. I was shaking and praying at the same time. One of the ladies accompanied me. Walking up the driveway was like climbing Mt. Everest. We noticed a man in the garage tinkering with something. So we went up to the garage. He came to the doorway with a smile. When I identified myself as representing the local Seventh-day Adventist Church, he exploded! I don't know if it was the word *church*, or *Seventh-day Adventist*, or both—but I set him off, big time. He told us, in no uncertain terms, to get off his property. We turned on our heels and left immediately. And that was my introduction to door-to-door work. Needless to say, it is not high on my ministry list.

There were other highlights that week, but the Holy Spirit saved the biggest for the end. During the week, a camaraderie developed in the group. Everybody seemed to know that something extra special was happening. People were staying up after the evening worship to pray and fellowship. Though I was tired, the fellowship was too good to miss. It's hard to explain, but there just seemed to be something different about our prayers and Scripture sharing.

The closing event was a communion service preceded by a foot washing. I've never experienced, before or after, what happened there. The Holy Spirit sent an extra touch of rain! Everybody knew it. There was a joy and unity among the group members that was inspiring. It's hard to put into words; words just aren't adequate to express it. I made a couple of life-long friends that week. Thirty-five years later, almost every time we run into each other or talk on the phone, that communion is brought up. What a joy to reminisce with old friends about something that is so rare in this world! It surely was a foretaste of Heaven. I was able to attend the next three LETSs at Soquel. They were very good, but they lacked the intensity of the Holy Spirit that was present in the first one. It was a rare occasion, when God chose to reveal Himself to that degree. I was humbled, and blessed, to have been part of it.

I returned on a spiritual high that lasted for a day or so. Then life wedged its way back into my reality. After a peak spiritual blessing like LETS, it is typical that, as I re-entered everyday life—with all the responsibilities, problems, and chaos—I would have a letdown. The blues, as it were. I have experienced this several times after prayer conferences, camp meetings, trainings, etc. It seems the human condition is not able to maintain a spiritual high in our frail bodies.

There is a biblical precedence for this phenomenon. Elijah, the powerful prophet of God, experienced one of the greatest spiritual encounters recorded in Scripture. By faith alone, at Carmel, he stood up to 450 priests of Baal and was victorious. Yet afterward, he ran from one evil woman and ended up hiding in a cave, asking to die.

Prophets and Kings contains this insightful comment: "But a reaction such as frequently follows high faith and glorious success was pressing upon Elijah. He feared that the reformation begun on Carmel might not be lasting; and depression seized him. He had been exalted to Pisgah's top; now he was in the valley" (White, p. 161).

Though the events at LETS and the encounter with the Holy Spirit were worlds apart from Elijah's majestic experience, it presents a principle that has borne out in my life. A spiritual high *can* be followed by a valley experience, a feeling of discouragement and despair. Does God have a reason for allowing this type of trial? I believe He does. One of the most important things I needed, and still need, to learn was that my own power is not sufficient in the Christian journey. Though we need God's power for everything we do; for every beat of our heart, every breath we take, I needed to learn *only* God's power is sufficient to get me through the rough spots in life.

There have been times when there is nothing that I can do but lean totally on Jesus. That's not a bad place to be, actually. It's when, in my weakness, I see no other place to go except to Jesus, it is then and only then, that I am truly strong.

> And He said to me, "My Grace is sufficient for you, for My strength is made perfect in weakness." Therefore most gladly I will rather boast in my infirmities, that the power of Christ may rest upon me. Therefore I take pleasure in infirmities, in reproaches, in needs, in persecutions, in distresses, for Christ's sake. *For when I am weak, then I am strong.* (2 Cor. 12: 9–10, emphasis added)

When it is hard to see Him, when there seems to be darkness, is when I have to rely on the spiritual tools that God offers us, His sinful, erring children. One of the most powerful tools in this type of trial is claiming Bible promises. When the pain is strong, when the tears are flowing, to have a sure promise like Hebrews 13:5: "I will *never* leave you nor forsake you," is a haven in the stormy trials of life (emphasis added). You can trust promises like that. Biblical faith is believing even when you can't perceive Jesus is there.

> *One of the most important things I needed, and still need, to learn was that my own power is not sufficient in the Christian journey.*

"For the disheartened there is a sure remedy—faith, prayer, work. Faith and activity will impart assurance and satisfaction that will increase day by day. Are you tempted to give way to feelings of anxious foreboding or utter despondency? In the darkest days, when appearances seem most forbidding, fear not. *Have faith in God*. He knows your need. He has all power. His infinite love and compassion never weary. Fear not that He will fail of *fulfilling His promise*. He is eternal truth" (*Prophets and Kings*, p.164, emphasis added).

So after giving myself a few days to regain my emotional bearings, I gave a report to the pastor. I thanked him for sending me. To this day, many years later, I am still grateful that God allowed me to encounter the Holy Spirit in such a way. If receiving a few showers of the Spirit brought such joy, what will the latter rain of the Spirit be like? I learned so much about the breadth of God's vast ministry and the gifts He gives to each one of us, if we are willing, in lifting up Jesus and helping others.

I continued to help the pastor with his duties. I was learning, enjoying it, too. I'm not sure what happened, but I began to entertain thoughts about whether God might be calling me to the ministry. Nothing else seemed to be happening in regard to a vocation. I began praying regularly about it. No answer came, so I continued helping the pastor and doing my other duties at home and church. Life was moving along; God was blessing in my studies and teaching. But I kept thinking about what kind of employment or ministry God had in mind. *What is the holdup, Lord?* I still had to learn that when *I thought* nothing particular was happening in my life, God was always working quietly, and powerfully, on His plans for me.

8.

A Divine Appointment

Heavenly Father, I just come to praise You and give You great glory. You are the great God of the universe, my Creator and the re-Creator of my heart. You are the Holy One of Israel, the One altogether lovely. I want to be in Your presence in the heavenly sanctuary. I come just as I am, a fool and a sinner. I have nothing to offer but my great need of You. I need to talk to You. I need to hear from You. I've been seeking You for a while. You know what I am seeking. I fully admit that I deserve nothing from You. But You are such a tremendous God. You forgive my sins and throw them into the depths of the sea. I know you have a plan for me, a plan to give me hope and a future. I claim that promise, I thank you for it. I believe it. But, Lord, You know that I struggle with impatience. How much longer until You open a door? How much longer until I see a clear path. It seems my life has been stuck for quite a while. Help me to wait on You, for I know Your timing is perfect. In Jesus' name, Amen!

And so, a steady stream of prayers like that ascended to the throne in heaven. There were many of them. I must have filled up one of those "golden bowls," which hold "the prayers of the saints" (see Rev. 5:8) in the heavenly sanctuary. Prayer assaults are great, but they aren't meant to change God's mind. In this instance, prayer was to help me search my heart and to clarify my motives. By my persistent prayers, I gave evidence of my strong confidence in God.

This prayer offensive continued from early spring through late summer. I felt that I needed an answer, a way forward. I was wrestling with my thoughts about whether God was calling me to the ministry. Here I was, in my mid-thirties, and divorced. It seemed a bit late to go through the scholastic course to become a pastor in our denomination. And I wasn't even a fair student. Greek, Hebrew? You've got to be kidding! But it was the only idea rolling around in my mind. In the past, I had read a story in *Adventist Review* about someone older than me who was called to the ministry. So I knew it was possible. I continued to pray. What else could I do?

Late summer in the Central California Conference meant Soquel Camp Meeting. A ten-day convocation of worship, great preaching, Bible classes (for all ages), health seminars, fellowship, and food. The campground is located just outside Santa Cruz, California, in a little town called Soquel. For decades it was situated on the beach. Then after World War II, the church purchased a plot of land from the US Army for a song. It had a number of buildings on it, including a very large one that was turned into an auditorium that can hold thousands of worshipers. I was eager to go. I secured a spot that was open in one of the "tent cities." The camp meeting was a huge undertaking, with hundreds of tents, RV and trailer parking, and cook houses spread around the campground. Almost all of the physical work was done by the pastors of the conference and numerous volunteers.

That's one reason I wanted to go: more than a hundred pastors would be there! I thought that I would talk to as many pastors as I could over the ten days. I hoped Jesus would give me some indication, some sign, of whether my echoing thoughts about the ministry were from Him. These types of situations can be difficult for me. *Self* has a strong desire to get its way. And since I had been chafing about my lack of work or new career, I needed to be extremely careful. Sometimes, when my human desire is strong, I need to take a step back, pray, and "wait patiently for the Lord" (see Psalm 40:1). Unfortunately, I can, by my impatient choices, get in the way of God's plan. Fortunately, His plan always has a way of coming to fruition. I make things harder for myself by letting my selfishness get its way.

During the time leading up to camp meeting, I had a growing understanding of the pitfalls of my own desires and impatience. Actually, I had begun my prayer offensive even before camp meeting was advertised. When I heard about camp meeting and realized there would be many pastors there, I began narrowing my prayers to focus on Soquel. For months I had put in the prayer time; I should have been at peace as I came to Soquel.

But I wasn't. I had a plan that *I thought* needed to occur while there. I felt I needed *this* to happen; I needed *that* information to materialize. I hadn't quite learned yet that I could be at peace in every situation. Jesus is still working with me on that one. God has a plan for every circumstance. He knew my heart; He knew I wanted to follow His plan. But self is always lurking, and the adversary knew how to use my impatience and selfish desires to break my peace. This was an area of growth that had a long way to go. Decades later, I can say that Jesus has been very good to me. By His grace He has patiently decreased my selfishness and impatience, and that has led to increased peace in my life. That's the type of God He is!

So I came to camp meeting with *my* plan, a plan that seemed right *to me* for finding out if God was calling me to the ministry. I am a blessed man. Even though I thought I had a plan God could bless, in His mercy He interposed and set *His* plan in motion. God is extremely merciful to me because I am a stubborn, hardheaded fool. Maybe it is because He knows my heart's desire. He knows I want to follow Him all the way to the earth made new. But I stumble so badly most of the time, and this was one of those times. I prayed inside of my car before I left for Soquel. I claimed one of my favorite promises, Psalm 32:8–9:

> I will instruct you and teach you in the way you should go; I will guide you with My eye. Do not be like the horse *or* like the mule, *which* have no understanding, *which* must be harnessed with bit and bridle, else they will not come near you.

Well, yes, I wanted to have Jesus teach me the way to go and guide me with His eye. Of course that was my plan. But because of *my plan* I also fit into the second part of the promise because I wasn't harnessed with a bit and bridle.

In my story, I have identified a couple of instances when Jesus stepped in to help me with a critical choice. A crossroads in my life, so to speak. The outcome of those choices took me in a whole different direction from what I was anticipating. There are points in my journey with Jesus where He sees that certain situations *must* occur for His plan to move forward. If those previous choices had been different, I don't know where I would be today.

I arrived at Soquel early on Thursday, to check in, unload my car at my tent, and look forward to ten days of a spiritual adventure. I spent some time in prayer, still praying about *my* plan and asking Jesus to bless it. I began exploring the campground, which was very large. Many people were rolling into the entrance with camper vans, trailers, and RVs of all sizes. They were backed up for quite a distance. I didn't know that this camp meeting was so large. I was thankful that I had arrived early and had only my car. I saw someone carrying groceries and realized I needed to do some shopping because I hadn't brought much to eat. Fortunately, there was a small grocery store with an area where all the veggie products were sold, a cafeteria, and a (veggie) burger bar run by kids from nearby

Monterrey Bay Academy. There was even a large ABC Bookstore occupying a massive room. It seemed like a little town had sprung up.

When I arrived back at my tent, I finished setting it up. I was amazed at how creative my neighbors were in setting up their tents. Some were luxurious with many amenities, compared to my sleeping bag, folding chairs, and card table. Fortunately, the camp provided bunks and a mattress that looked like they were from World War II. I went looking for the bathrooms and was surprised to see the rows of cabins (for seniors) that had housed everybody during the LETS training event, months before. The grounds looked so different, with the numerous large tents that had been set up for the children's divisions. There was a super large tent for the Spanish meetings. There were also smaller tents for some health ministries. As the RVs rolled in and more people arrived, the camp took on a different atmosphere from when I had been there at LETS, with only a few people.

That night, I attended the opening meeting, in the cavernous main auditorium. Since it was Thursday night, attendance was minimal. I didn't realize that all the camping vehicles I had seen were only a fraction of the vehicles that would be arriving the following day, when people got off work for the weekend. Even though the attendance was sparse, it was an excellent meeting. Great music, remarkable testimonies, and powerful preaching. I went to bed that night with anticipation about what was going to happen in the days to come. And what I might find about my future. I must say, I really found out!

The next day was Friday. After breakfast I went for a walk, hoping to begin talking to some pastors about what was on my heart. A couple of things happened that got in the way of satisfying my desire. The first one was caused by the sheer busyness of the camp as people rolled in to register. The pastors did everything from welcoming, directing people to the registration booth, helping people to their site, and guiding drivers as they backed into very small spots. I really appreciated their dedication and expertise. They must have been praying, because I saw two incidents in which seemingly oversized trailers were somehow maneuvered into extremely difficult sites. There was no way I could interfere with their difficult, important work. The other thing that got in the way of my agenda was the overall program. There were extensive classes, seminars, prayer meetings, preaching, and free health screenings scheduled back-to-back throughout the day, starting at 6:30 a.m. I was drawn to everything. Add to that, finding time to eat, keeping your tent clean, and other activities of daily living. That first couple of days I ran around like the proverbial chicken with his head cut off.

I decided I wouldn't make it through the ten days at this pace. I had to slow down. But there were so many things to do. It was fun and exciting. So I took the program of events and prayerfully mapped out a schedule. That helped to slow me down, but God had other plans. In my "tent neighborhood" I met a couple of women, nurses. I struck up a conversation with one while I helped them tighten the ropes to adjust their tent. In the midst of our conversation, she started talking about changing her career. She talked about going back to school to become a counselor because she might be burning out on nursing and needed a new direction. This led to a conversation about some of my experiences with people over the last couple of years and how inadequate I was when people would reveal their painful experiences to me. She pointed out the need for counselors in the church. She shared some information concerning pastors being overwhelmed with the counseling portion of their ministry. Research, she said, showed that the average pastor had only one or two classes in counseling during their time at various seminaries. Marriage counseling was at the top of their list of frustrations.

> *It always amazes me how God can blend situations together to bring out His plans.*

This interested me and I put it in the back of my mind. We then spent the remainder of our conversation on sorting out her needs and on the logistics of making the transition from nursing to counseling. We had a prayer for direction in her journey and went our separate ways. I thought it had just been a conversation meeting her needs, but I didn't realize God was beginning to reveal the answer to my mountain of prayers. It always amazes me how God can blend situations together to bring out His plans. It seemed her needs were met, and that God had begun trying to get my attention. Sometimes it is difficult to get through to me, but God has His ways. He can be very persistent.

I was having a peak spiritual experience and a lot of fun. But I noticed I wasn't getting to the most important reason I was there. I wasn't talking to any pastors. I found it a little difficult to determine who was a pastor among all the men doing the work around the camp. They were so busy. The camp was very old, so many things needed maintenance and there were constant emergencies—pipes breaking, electricity going out, septic problems, etc. The camp's systems struggled to handle the sudden influx of thousands of people. If I would start a conversation with a pastor, someone or something would interrupt us.

So I would give up, telling myself that I had plenty of time remaining in the week. Plus, I *had* to move on because the afternoon seminar was beginning. Off I would go, running to class. I truly loved being in the camp-meeting atmosphere. There was so much to do without interference from the world. This was before cell phones were prevalent, so if you wanted, you could leave the world and its problems behind for ten days.

One of the things I found appealing was the variety of ethnic groups at the camp. It was truly a fulfillment of the calling of the three angels' messages to take the gospel "to every nation, tribe, tongue, and people" (Rev. 14:6). I was seeing this fulfillment on a smaller scale at the Japanese church every Sabbath, but the message was demonstrated in a much broader measure at Soquel. People, some in their native garb, could be seen all over the campground, especially in the cookhouses. Though I had no cookware, I found myself in one of the kitchens, often. The aromas were a magnet to my gastrointestinal system as I would walk by. With microwaves and a dozen or so burners in use and a number of women from various cultures tending to their recipes, a veritable smorgasbord appeared throughout the day. And yes, on occasion, I was offered a taste or two of great ethnic vegetarian cooking.

It always amazes me how Jesus can blend the normal activities of our day to bring about divine appointments. One day I stuck my head in one of the cookhouses. It wasn't crowded, so I entered. There was a young lady washing dishes while some kind of savory dish simmered nearby. I immediately knew I was supposed to talk with her. It is hard to explain how I knew, but I just knew. With ease we started a conversation that lasted, on and off, for more than fifteen years! It must have been the Spirit's revealing, but I knew she was in great need. This was different from the other times I talked to women. I didn't feel the inadequacy that I'd felt in the past. Without any prodding on my part, she opened up. We ended up talking for a long time outside the cookhouse. In fact, we ended up talking and praying several times during the camp. She was carrying deep wounds. She needed to talk. Jesus was doing the "therapy" because I didn't know what to do. She must have benefitted because, at the end of the camp meeting, she asked if we could keep in touch. We did.

From time to time, one or the other of us would call. She struggled for several years. I felt that I was just along for the ride, which was quite bumpy for her. She finally started some long-term therapy. It seemed to help her because, when we would talk, I could hear something new in her voice: hope. After a few years had passed, I bumped into her at a conference. She looked like a new woman—smiling, animated, vibrant. We picked up like no time had passed since we had talked last. She was volunteering at an elementary school in a program that identified at-risk kids. She would simply "play" with the kids in a playroom the school set up through a state-funded program. It was life-changing for her. It was with great satisfaction that I acknowledged that Jesus was doing a work in her. She agreed.

I didn't hear from her for a couple of years, then she called to tell me she had gone back to school to become a clinical social worker, a counselor. We talked a few times while she was in school and struggling with a certain class or assignment. About all I could do was encourage her and pray for God's blessing. She graduated, eventually received her license, and went into private practice. Then difficulties arose. We talked more often after she got married. Marriage has a way of bringing out the best and worst of a person. For a couple of more years, I felt I was again along for the ride as her marriage deteriorated. She found out she had married a closet alcoholic and struggled with all that can mean in a marriage. I saw her one more time at Soquel a couple of years later. The difficult marriage had taken its toll. She was divorced, and the wounds weren't healing well. We lost track after that. She's one I will be looking for in the earth made new. Come, Lord Jesus!

So, there I was, simply wanting to satisfy my senses by stopping by one of the cookhouses. But God had a plan. I didn't stop there by chance; He had set up an appointment, an appointment to help someone in need. And not only that, to give me more evidence, He was answering my prayers about my future. Since I had been focusing on finding out about a call to the ministry, what started in that cookhouse didn't set off any fireworks in my mind to alert me that God was leading in another direction. At that time, I was kind of narrow minded, focused on what *I thought* needed to happen. Jesus knew this and patiently kept working on me to get my attention. He is the master psychologist and He knows the absolute best way to work with my heart and mind. After many years, I have a growing confidence that I can trust Jesus with the very inner recesses of my heart. He stands at the door [of our hearts] and knocks (see Rev. 3:20). But we must open the door to let Him in.

Jesus made another attempt to get my attention by setting up another divine appointment. I met a man while standing in line at the burger bar.

As what seems to happen when Jesus is leading, we quickly fell into a conversation, which led to our eating lunch together. This young man had a work-related problem. Since I had been in business management, it was easy to understand the dynamics of his situation. He was afraid that if the problem were not resolved, he could lose his job. He was fearful because of borderline financial problems that could explode if he lost his job. We talked about several issues and, for some reason, I asked him about his tithing practices. He admitted he needed to clean up the way he handled God's money. After a while, we had prayer and went our separate ways. I ran into him once more, later in the week. We had some more prayer and he thanked me for my interest.

God was calling, but I wasn't answering. I must have not been listening. The wooing of the Spirit can be quite gentle, but quite persistent. I should have realized something was up with these occurrences. The nurse, the cookhouse appointment, the man with a work problem. But for some reason, they didn't. Jesus knew this was the time to answer the mountain of prayers that I had built up, so He tried another avenue. Jesus is so wise and compassionate. It was getting along on this ten-day journey at Soquel.

Finally, I fell into a situation where I was able to talk to a pastor without getting interrupted. He was an older man who had been in the ministry for a while. We met in the corner of what was called the small auditorium, which was near the bookstore on the campground. It was in between seminars, so it was relatively quiet. We had prayer, then I laid out why I wanted to talk to him. He was very attentive and gave good feedback and information about becoming a pastor. He was a bit concerned, as I had been, about my age. But He knew others who had become pastors later in life. He answered every question and then some. He was wise, asking about my background. A thought flashed into my mind at the last moment. I told him about the information the nurse had shared with me about pastors being overwhelmed in portions of their ministry because of their lack of expertise in counseling. He heartily confirmed that was true. He went on to say he had considered going back to school earlier in his ministry. We ended with prayer and I headed for the burger bar.

While eating, I contemplated my visit with the pastor. He was very helpful and gave me all the time I needed. I tried to review what he had said while it was fresh in my mind. There really wasn't anything that stuck out to me. I guess I was hoping for a bolt of lightning or something along those lines. I needed some clear direction, a spotlight on my path. By the end of my burger, I was ready to find another pastor to see if there was a "word from the Lord" out there for me. But the evening meeting was starting, and I didn't want to miss the opening testimony time. I became engrossed and forgot about looking for another pastor. I have to admit I felt less motivated to find another one that night. After the meeting, I went back to my tent and had a good night's rest.

It was getting late in the ten-day schedule and I had talked to only one pastor. Early the next morning, I decided to skip the 6:30 meeting to spend some extra time in prayer, seeking God's direction. I told Him I was sorry for not being more diligent in finding pastors. With only four days left, I humbled myself before Him. I asked His forgiveness and told Him I knew He was going to lead me to the information I needed. I wasn't dictating, I was trying to exhibit faith in *His plan* for me. It was becoming apparent, while praying, that *my plan* wasn't necessarily His plan. I just needed to find out what His plan was. I felt I *really* needed to have an answer about my future. I was wrestling with God. As I continued to pray, a promise came forcefully to mind. One that was perfect for my situation. God is very merciful to me. It was originally given to the prophet Jeremiah while he was in prison. "Call to Me, and I will answer you, and show you great and mighty things, which you do not know" (Jer. 33:3). Wow! That was very comforting. I was calling out in prayer. I was needing an answer, but to what, I didn't know. And God promised to clear up my lack of understanding. Praise God! My faith was strengthened and as I got up from my knees; I was surprised to see the time. It was mid-morning.

After squeezing in the door, just as they were closing, I grabbed a quick breakfast at the cafeteria. Then I went into the main auditorium where the morning seminars were drawing to a close. I caught the last few minutes of one. Something the lady who was leading said, captured my attention. Then the class broke up and I started to go to my next scheduled event. I briefly thought about talking to the lady about what had caught my attention, but she was surrounded by people asking questions. I stashed my question away for another time.

Next, I went to a group prayer time that was offered, and joined with the others to praise and honor God. Group prayer is very important. God promises to answer our prayers, and He does. We are encouraged to pray in large and small groups along with private prayer. Group prayer seems to open a channel that private prayer does not. I have been encouraged by this statement about group prayer: "The promise is made on the condition that the united prayers of the church are offered, and in answer to these prayers there may be expected a *power greater than that which comes in answer to private prayer*" (White, *Manuscript Releases*, vol. 9, p. 303, emphasis added). Wow! The ultimate Biblical example of the power of group prayer is the upper-room experience at Pentecost.

The day passed quickly, and I still hadn't talked to a pastor. I ended the day dejected and wondering if I was getting in the way of God's working out His plan, or if I didn't really want an answer. I was confused. Then a verse came to mind: "God is not *the author* of confusion but of peace" (1 Cor. 14:33). This verse was timely, helpful. If God is not the author of confusion, then the adversary must be lurking. My courage was strengthened and my faith restored that God would answer my mountain of prayers.

I had a new thought. Something that I hadn't considered: *Maybe it wasn't in God's plan to answer my prayers at camp meeting.* Maybe, in His wisdom, it wasn't the best time. Because I was so focused on receiving an answer that *I wanted*, and my impatience had caused my vision to narrow, could I be mistaken about when He would answer my prayers? Or was the answer to be delayed? In one of his books, the pastor-evangelist Glenn Coon said something to the effect that God promises to answer our prayers, but He reserves the right to answer when He knows it's best. His timing is perfect, mine is not, because of my selfish desires. This possibility kept me awake that night. But the confusion was gone, and I felt renewed peace that God was in control. This new perspective enabled me to totally let go of my narrow, selfish agenda. He would answer at the perfect time. This was a big lesson for me. Don't let selfish desires limit God. After all, He *is* God! I was going to finish camp meeting and enjoy whatever came along. God had a plan!

I felt so much better the next day, as if a burden had been taken off my back. I think it was the best day of camp meeting. Nothing particular happened that morning; I just felt a lightness that brought me great joy. God was in control. I realized that I was doing myself in, earlier in the week, because I was trying to make *my agenda* happen. Because of my natural self wanting its own way, I was placing myself in restraints. It was wonderful to realize that even amidst my selfish desires and mistakes God is still working out His plan. Praise God!

Late in the afternoon, after the seminars had ended for the day, the large auditorium would be relatively quiet until the evening meeting started. I liked to sit in there during that time and relax and pray. That afternoon, I noticed a couple sitting down across the way. I recognized the woman as the person who was leading the seminar I had sat in on for a few minutes the day before. I still had a question about something she had said in the few minutes I was there. I debated whether I should bother her. Sometimes people who lead seminars can get tired of answering questions all week. I decided to ask but not take up much of her time. I prayerfully crossed the auditorium and approached the couple.

I introduced myself and inquired if I could ask my question. She was very open to talking, and asked me to sit down. She introduced herself and her husband. She said they were from Berrien Springs, Michigan. I asked if she worked at Andrews University, which is located there. She said no, but that they were both affiliated with the university. I asked them in what way. The Holy Spirit washed over me as she answered. I couldn't believe it. She said that they were both licensed counselors! I broke out laughing, I couldn't help it. I was electrified. Once again, when God's time has come, nothing, absolutely nothing, can stop it. The Spirit hit me like a ton of bricks.

After I apologized for my outburst, we fell into a lengthy conversation. They were very attentive. I explained why I was laughing. I told them this must be a divine appointment. I must have come across as a chattering fool. My mind was spinning; I thought my heart was going to burst. I wonder what they were thinking.

I briefly outlined some details about the last few years of my life. Then I focused on my struggles with where my life was going and finding out what God's plan was for me. They asked a few questions (as any counselor would), which helped clarify my statements. Then I focused on the reasons I had come to Soquel and the situations that had happened here at camp meeting, the people I had talked to.

Jesus *must* have been leading these two. Everything they said was right to the point and spoke to my heart. One of them wondered if maybe Jesus was trying to call me to be a counselor instead of a pastor. Wow! It was as if scales fell from my eyes. Since my divorce, God had been gently showing me—by sending people into my life—that he was calling me to be a counselor. I hadn't seen it. I just hadn't seen it! I think being dull-minded and hardheaded had something to do with my not catching it. I wasn't very in tune with the Holy Spirit back then. I was a babe. Even before I left Chico, with my friend asking me for help with a problem, God was leading me in that direction. Being approached by various people at churches in the Bay Area, God was leading me in that direction. The newly licensed marriage and family counselor who vigorously told me I needed to go back to school and become a counselor. The Adventist singles conference with the Christian counselors. Not to mention the people I had talked with at

Soquel. And I'm sure there were instances of other signs I didn't pick up on. Yes, God was leading me in that direction.

Time passed rapidly and I suggested we bring things to a close. They agreed and said something that I had heard before, "You should go back to school and become a counselor." We had prayer and they left for dinner. I sat there in that cavernous auditorium, stunned and weakened from the encounter. Wow! God is powerful! I mumbled a short prayer of thanksgiving and slouched in my chair. I set for a while and tried to let my mind go blank. I just needed to relax and pull things back together.

After a while, I was brought back to the moment by the sound of people clanging chairs as they set up for the evening meeting. As I walked back to my tent, I was beginning to piece together what had just happened. God had been faithful in answering my prayers. Not in the way I expected, but in the way He knew was best. I didn't go to the evening meeting that night because I wanted to assess what had transpired, and I was worn out. It wasn't so much a physical fatigue as an emotional/spiritual fatigue. I guess an encounter with the Holy Spirit can have that kind of effect. It was very different from the communion experience at LETS. That was a more powerful, outward, joyful experience. This was a more personal, impactful experience; a wake-up call. I'm no expert on the working of the Holy Spirit, but it seems He can manifest Himself in different ways to bring about the results He wants.

He certainly knew what He was doing with me in this encounter. I was deeply humbled as I realized how much time and energy I had spent praying about *my plan*. Especially the angst and worry. If I had been more mature in my walk with Jesus, I would have had a great deal more peace as I sought His will for my future. So had all the time I spent in prayer about my plan been a waste of time? No. Never! Any time spent in the presence of God is beneficial; it is life changing. He is the great Power in the universe; the One who holds all things together; the One whose love and mercy is so great that He allowed His own Son to die for us.

9.

The Enemy's PhD

What can I say about my God? No! What can I shout about Him? Words, sometimes, don't suffice because they cannot express what the heart is proclaiming in praise! Once I was back at my tent and getting myself together, I tried assessing what had just happened with those two counselors. As I reviewed the way Jesus lined up the circumstances, from the timing to the words, I was overwhelmed by God's greatness. And He manifested that greatness and power for me—for my benefit! I was astonished.

> I will extol You, my God, O King; And I will bless Your name forever and ever. Every day I will bless You, and I will praise your name forever and ever. Great *is* the LORD, and greatly to be praised; And His greatness *is* unsearchable. (Ps. 145:1–3)

Yes, God is great, far beyond my understanding. Why should I deserve such blessings? Why would the God of the universe manifest His mercy and power for a stubborn sinner like me? Why? Because He loves me and knows that I am truly helpless. He knows me thoroughly; He "searches my heart" completely (see Ps. 139:1, 23). He knows who I am. He remembers how weak I am. He knows that I am "dust" (Ps. 103:14). I am blessed beyond measure to know such a merciful God.

Leading up to Soquel, my predominantly selfish nature caused me to have a narrow view of my life, a self-centered understanding of what I needed. It was like lacking peripheral vision, not being able to see the full scope of the possibilities there are with Jesus. But He understood me; He knew I needed help as I stumbled along the way. And He was willing and able to guide me. I think of this text: "I will bring the blind by a way they did not know; I will lead them in paths they have not known. I will make darkness light before them, and crooked places straight. These things I will do for them, and not forsake them" (Isa. 42:16).

I am humbled and broken as I contemplate this fourfold promise and apply it to my situation at camp meeting. Jesus promises to fulfill these promises. And He did, big time! Isaiah's proclamation is a promise that covers many avenues in which Jesus could help me.

1. No matter how blind I was to Jesus' answering my mountain of prayers, He promised to lead me on a path I didn't know. A walk on that path leading to faith and trust. I'm still learning that one.
2. He promised to bring light to my darkness, which had obscured His leading. How many times did Jesus give indication of His will for me? It seems that my darkness was so deep, He had to use a bright spotlight, right there in the large auditorium at Soquel.
3. He promised to give me a straight path to understand His guidance. I certainly needed that! That need remains today.
4. The promise to "not forsake" me is one of the most precious promises in Scripture for me. Knowing that Jesus is there in *every* situation brings peace, joy, and gratitude. Hallelujah!

I have learned, without a shadow of doubt, that I can apply each and every promise God has made to me, personally. That is, there are thousands of promises that I can make my own. One of the reasons the promises are in the Scriptures is to help me learn that Jesus can be trusted in every circumstance of life. He wants to be trusted. He *can* be trusted! The promises, and their fulfillment, along with providential leadings, and the power of Scripture, are what Jesus uses to develop my faith. Jesus is a near God. He is an interested God. He is a personal God. He hungers for me to open my heart to Him. He longs to come in, and I have learned to open the door and let Him in.

The next day was Sabbath, the last full day of camp meeting. What a day for me to lift up praise and adoration to God. The perception of my life was completely changed. There was a lightness, a joy, a peace that passes all understanding. The mission, the determination I had when I arrived at Soquel, was gone. Jesus had been faithful; He had manifested Himself in a clear and dynamic way. He had broken down the mistaken conviction I had arrived with. Because of my presumption concerning the reason for my stay at Soquel, Jesus knew that a direct demonstration would be needed to get through to me. He truly fulfilled the promise that I claimed upon leaving home. He really did "instruct me and teach me in the way I should go" (Ps. 32:8).

So far, my story testifies to the tenacity, the relentless pursuit that Jesus will take on to help a sinner like me. He truly is "The Hound of

Heaven," as the English poet Francis Thompson said in his poem of the same name, which centers on the pursuit of a sinner by a loving God.

The Sabbath passed quickly, without any more fireworks. The day before, it seemed, Jesus had completed what He knew had to happen in order to answer my prayers. My true prayers. The prayers of the inner recesses of my heart. My heart's desire. The apostle Paul tells us that we sinners don't even know what to pray for. A merciful, gracious promise in Romans says, "Likewise the Spirit also helps in our weaknesses. *For we do not know what we should pray for* as we ought, but the Spirit Himself makes intercession for us with groanings which cannot be uttered" (Rom. 8:26, emphasis added).

To me, this means when my prayers ascend to the heavenly sanctuary, the Spirit transforms those prayers and makes them more acceptable to God. Those mountains of prayers that ascended before camp meeting were mercifully "upgraded" by the Spirit to what was in my heart of hearts. I am so grateful that Jesus understands me thoroughly; He knows my inner recesses. He knows, despite my inborn selfishness, what I really want. *And what I really want is all that God has planned for me.* I have learned that His plan comes with a price, a cheap price at that, which is not fulfilling my selfish desires.

The situation at Soquel is only one example of the struggle I have with living my life with Jesus. Self tells me one thing; the Spirit and the Scripture tell me different. I have learned, through the Spirit, to disregard most of my desires and rely on what God says. It is true, after many years of walking with Jesus, that He has been, and still is, changing my selfish desires. This stubborn sinner has learned a few things, finally. But I still have a long, long way to go. With Jesus, I am confident that He will walk with me as far as I need to go, which is eternal life.

I woke up on Sunday, the last day of camp meeting, to the noises of camp breaking. People taking down their tents, packing their equipment, and saying goodbye. This was the first time I was happy I hadn't brought more furnishings. Some were having to throw away some of their stuff because of lack of space in their vehicles. I was amazed by how much purchasing some people had done. Cases of veggie food, books, and Sabbath School materials filled up their vehicles.

Though many were rushed to get on the road, with lengthy travel ahead, I still had a couple of things to do. Living only about thirty minutes from Soquel enabled me to spend a leisurely morning. Not everybody was finished with their camp. A dedicated dentist was still seeing patients at the health tent. A retired senior citizen, he was donating his expertise during the camp. Late in the week, I had decided to have a free exam and was fortunate to get one of his last appointments that Sunday morning. I have had very few problems with my teeth, so the exam went well. When he was finished and his next appointment hadn't shown up yet, he struck up a conversation with me. He asked if I had received any special blessings during camp.

I told the dentist a short version of what had happened and told him that I felt Jesus was calling me to be a counselor. For some reason, my little story set him off. He became animated and loud. He started moving around the little tent and doing a little jig. Speaking rapidly, he told me about how much the church needed counselors—how there were so many problems, most pastors didn't have the time to tend to them. Things I had been hearing on and off for a couple of years. But his enthusiasm was impactful. His next patient showed up in the midst of this, and was quite amused. He ended our time with a prayer for success in my calling. My head was spinning as I walked back to my tent. What was that all about!? As always, Jesus knew what He was doing. He knew an attack from the adversary was imminent.

I arrived back at my tent still contemplating my conversation with the dentist. I packed my meager gear and brought my car around to clear out. I borrowed a broom, swept the tent out one more time, and loosened the ropes to help the volunteers who would come by later to fold it up and take it away. These people were very organized in their work. It reminded me of the picture the Old Testament paints of the Israelites as they wandered in the desert for forty years. They were very organized as they moved a multitude of people from place to place. They were especially careful as they moved the tabernacle. God is a God of order.

I had a prayer of thanksgiving for the miracles of answered prayer and the blessings of camp. As I slowly exited with the mobile homes, RVs, and trailers, my mind began assimilating what had happened during Soquel. Somewhere ahead of me, a breakdown or accident brought the long line of campers to a halt. More time to think about the ramifications of becoming a counselor. As I sat waiting, I suddenly was overwhelmed with terror and anxiety. I began perspiring and shaking. What is going on? Jesus help me!

It didn't take long for me to understand. I had come to a realization of something, and that something gave an opening for the adversary to attack. If, in fact, Jesus was calling me to be a counselor, that would mean I would have to go back to school! *Horrors! Shock! Dread! Panic! Palpitations!* The list could go on and on. I was a basket case. It was a blessing that I was stuck in traffic.

I have already shared some of my past experience with education, of which I'm not proud. But the whole story needs to be told. Then it will be clearer why I was open to attack. It is one of the adversary's goals to attack sinners at their weakest point. He knows this is where our defenses are least effective. He knows he can enter like a flood, taking out everything in his path. There is an instructive statement concerning one of the ways the adversary works, in *Faith I Live By*: "The tempter has no power to control the will or to force the soul to sin. He may distress, but he cannot contaminate. He can cause agony, but not defilement. Satan cannot read our thoughts, but he can see our actions, hear our words; and from his long knowledge of the human family, he can shape his temptations to take advantage of our *weak points of character*" (White, p. 327, emphasis added).

The Adversary has a PhD in the human family. He's been in school for thousands of years. He knew that lifelong failure, shame, and wounds comprised my experience with formal education. He knew that as I sat in my car, he had an open shot at that weakness. Though he didn't know what I was thinking about, he had observed the incidents at camp. He heard what the two counselors said. He heard my testimony to the dentist. He knew a real trial would come when I was confronted with school. So he took the opportunity to attack. And attack he did. It was all I could do to hold it together. By pleading with God, I was able to calm myself and anxiously make it home once the traffic cleared up.

In thinking about how the adversary can attack humans, we must always keep this topic in the context of God's omniscience. He knows everything that is happening in this world to each one of us, and at all times, too, a very comforting truth. The adversary can do only what God allows him to do, and nothing more. The first two chapters of Job offer the prime example of how this works. God knows my weak points, those wounds that I carry. Part of the growing process is to be tested, tempted, and tried. Going faithfully through these trials *with Jesus* leads me to healing and growing in my faith. Thus, these situations are part of the healing, sanctifying process. In times like those I was experiencing, I needed to remember that the adversary is a thrice-defeated foe. He was first defeated in the war that broke out in heaven (see Rev. 12:7). He was defeated a second time when Jesus beat the adversary in the temptation in the wilderness (see Matt. 4) and a third time when Jesus died on the cross. Amen! The adversary is a spent particle compared to the great God of the universe. "He who is in you is greater than he who is in the world" (1 John 4:4).

What is my backstory concerning education, that allowed the adversary to attack? My parents were Depression-era folk. Just common, small-town Midwesterners who had little formal education. They didn't have the opportunity for much schooling, but they were part of the moral fabric of our country that made it so great. They were hardworking, honest people who wanted to make life better for their family. But they didn't know how to motivate me, how to give me educational skills and resources, or impress me with the importance of being educated. They both had to work to maintain our lower middle-class status.

The elementary school I attended had three classes for each grade. One class was for the high achievers, one for the average students, and one for those with difficulty learning. I was always in the average class. In that environment I struggled. I had difficulty staying focused in class. I was always caught gazing out the window, usually watching the kids playing outside. Today, I would probably be given a diagnosis of ADD. I was called a "dreamer." The most important outcome of that style of grouping young students is the powerful message it gives. The message is, *I am average and should not expect much of myself*. Or, *Don't expect to go far in life*. To elementary-school kids, these are powerful spoken and unspoken messages that embed deeply in their subconscious.

After several years of barely getting by, I entered high school. Those early teen years can be the most difficult time in life because so much change is happening physically and emotionally. I was pretty immature. With the requirement of a C average to play sports, basketball and baseball, I found enough incentive to stay eligible for four years, barely. Finding out that I needed glasses to see the chalkboard and that allergy medications were causing me to fall asleep in class only added to my struggles. Due to a case of "senioritis," I really shouldn't have graduated with my class because I let my grades drop below a C average. But I was pushed along. It didn't help that my school was given an award as the top academic public high school in California that year. Some of my best friends were high achievers. School was not for me. The shame of years of failure got the better of me.

With my grade point average, I qualified for admission only to the local Junior College, on probation. At the beginning of my story, I briefly acknowledged my several failures, which made it nearly impossible to advance toward a degree. Because of my fear, immaturity, and lack of interest, I was overwhelmed by the college atmosphere. It would have been the first college degree in my family. I was ready to quit when Jesus stepped into my life, unbeknownst to me, and caused a couple of miracles to happen that opened the way for me to go to Chico State University. I've already told part of that story. Even though I didn't know then that He existed, He was watching over me. He knew that I needed to get that bachelor's degree if I was going to qualify to study for a master's degree in counseling many years later. Jesus truly knows the end from the beginning. These academic failures left a deep wound in my soul. The adversary's scraping that old wound brought out the fear I experienced while leaving camp.

As I pulled into the parking garage of my mother's condo, I had a strong feeling that I was to go to San Jose State University and look into their counseling program. I trembled at the thought. I rebelled at the possibility. I sat in my car for quite a while and prayed and contemplated what my mountain of prayers might lead to. Could I get myself to do what God had told me to do? How could this possibly be the answer that I sought? Could I be mistaken about what had happened at camp meeting? All the shame and fear of a lifetime of educational failure overwhelmed me. I finally stowed my stuff from camp meeting and took the elevator up to the condo. Finding my mother doing well, I cleaned up and tried to get back into the routine of my life. As I mentioned earlier, coming home after a spiritual feast like camp meeting could be followed by a letdown; a period of the spiritual blahs. It didn't happen this time. I was so focused on the potential catastrophe that God had laid at my door that I had no down time.

I was tired, so I napped most of the afternoon. The following day was Monday, and I woke up wrestling with the situation, alternating between faith and fear. Fear was winning. I decided to fast and pray for the day. Fasting is a rare discipline for me. It is not on my agenda regularly. It is used as a way to alert God that I am coming to Him in earnest. He knows that if I am willing to give up food, I am in desperate need of help.

I decided to go to the university the next day to see what I could find out about the counseling program. Talk about trembling, talk about anxiety! I really didn't want to go. But my mountain of prayers reminded me of my desire to have some clarity about my future. I should have realized that Jesus had given me ample indication at camp meeting about His plan for my life. I shouldn't have had any hesitation, but fear causes questioning. After a lengthy worship, I talked myself into driving the few miles to the university. What could be so difficult about asking some questions?

Once again, God's time had come. I had no idea what was about to happen when I arrived at the university. I'm about to describe, as best I can remember, the absolutely awesome power of God in human events. My events!

San Jose State was a fairly large university in 1985, with about 20,000 students. It was mainly a commuter school, with few students staying on campus. This meant that parking was at a premium. As I took the freeway off-ramp, I was stressed, and prayed, Lord, help! Get me where you want me go. I had no idea where to go. "Your ears shall hear a word behind you, saying, 'This *is* the way, walk in it'" (Isa. 30:21). There were a few young people, probably students, who thought they could cross the street at any time and any place. I had to be very careful as I cruised along looking for, I didn't know what. I decided to find the next parking space and ask directions to the admissions office. There was somewhat of a circular loop around the campus. The first time I went around, I made a wrong turn and almost ended up back on the freeway. Part of me wanted to get back on the freeway and go home. But somehow I turned around and found my way back to campus. I went around the loop again with no success in finding a spot. I went around a third time with no parking in sight. I was really struggling. How can I find what You want me to find if I can't park?

I gave God one more chance. I told Him I would go around one more time and if there were no spot available, then I was going home. I felt four times around was enough. So I went around again and as I came out of a turn, I saw a space! It was a two-lane one-way street and I was in the correct lane to grab the spot. I parallel parked and sat there watching people go by. I remember the weather was out of the ordinary for a day in August. The sky was overcast, reflective of my mood. I didn't want to get out of the car. I wrestled with God and my fears. "perfect love casts out fear" (1 John 4:18). Right then I needed an abundance of Jesus' love just to get out of the car. I finally exited by grabbing hold of the promise in Isaiah, for guidance and by rationalizing that I was only looking for information.

When I climbed out of my car, I immediately saw the parking meter, which had a little sign on it that read *1 hr. parking. STRICTLY ENFORCED!* I thought that was strange because the meters on either side didn't have that sign. So I put in a coin and said, Okay, Jesus, You've got one hour. Where do I go from here? I looked at my watch as I turned around. One hour! To my shock, I turned around to face a sign on the building behind me that read *ADMISSIONS*. One parking spot—and it is right in front of where I needed to go? Stunned, I thanked Jesus for fulfilling His promise, "this is the way" (Isa. 30:21). It couldn't have been clearer. I strode, with trepidation, down the walkway toward the front door. A memory hit me from my sojourn years before at Chico State. Any administrative request or function on a college campus moves slowly. Administrative gears run slow. This memory calmed me briefly. What could I get done in one hour?

I entered; the lobby was empty. It was setup similar to that in a bank, with the employees behind a thin, wire mesh screen for security. There must have been a dozen spaces. Only two were open. One was occupied by a lady who finished her business and left as I walked up. I didn't think anything was out of the ordinary. Little did I know. As I walked up to the counter, I sent up a quick prayer for help, to ask the right questions. The young lady was bright and perky, asking, "How can I help you?"

I found myself blurting out that I was looking for information about the counseling program in the psychology department.

"I'm sorry, that program is full," was the response.

Music to my ears!

I stood there wondering what to say next when she said, "The program is already filled for the next three semesters." I didn't hear what she said after that. I was screaming inside with every fiber of my being, *I DON'T HAVE TO GO TO SCHOOL! I DON'T HAVE TO GO TO SCHOOL!* Oh, the emotional release. A real cathartic event. I barely acknowledged her as she asked me if I wanted to be put on the waiting list. I turned to go, when I was yanked back to reality by her words, "We have another counseling program, in the education department. Would like that information?"

Stunned, and with a modicum of fear returning, I found myself saying yes.

She gave me the application and other paperwork and directed me to the graduate-school office. It was in another part of the same building, so I found it easily. I walked into another empty office. It was much smaller than the Admissions section. The receptionist welcomed me with a smile. I haltingly stated why I was there. She immediately knew what to do and efficiently gave me some additional paperwork. I was just following along. Jesus, is this what is supposed to be happening? She also provided a campus map and gave me sketchy directions to the education department. She didn't know that maps and I don't get along. Being unfamiliar with the campus, even with the map, I had to ask a passing student for help. The

Counselor Education Department was on the other side of campus, on the second floor of the education building.

Once there, I found the dean's office. Again, the office was empty except for the secretary. I explained why I was there and asked what I needed to do. She replied, "Unfortunately, the dean is on vacation." My heart skipped a beat, and I was thrilled to my soul. I was looking for an out wherever I could find one. But reality crept back in when she continued, "The assistant dean is here and maybe he would have time to see you." She made a call and soon a small, older, balding man arrived and invited me into his office. As we walked down the hall, I wondered what he would say; what I would say? As we entered his office, he told me if I had been one minute later, He would have been gone for a few days of vacation. *One minute later!*

He asked me a number of questions about my academic record and my background, my life experience. I answered those questions and then I told him about some of the counseling-type situations I had experienced over the last couple of years. We talked about a few other incidental things. He took my name and other identifying information. Then he shocked me by saying, "Well, get your application turned in and I will make sure you are accepted."

Jesus had pulled off a major miracle! In fifty-four minutes, He had so arranged the series of events so as to open the way for me to complete what He wanted me to do.

I don't know what kind of outward reaction he saw, but inside I was in absolute chaos. *Jesus, what is going on? How can this be happening; I only came for some information. What am I going to do in Graduate School? Only the top students go to grad school!* What could I do but say I would do my best to meet the application requirements? I was a basket case as I left his office.

I found my way back to my car. As I unlocked the door, a question came to mind. I decided to run into the admissions office and ask someone. It would only take a minute. I looked at my watch and saw I had six minutes left on my hour parking. A shock like a bolt of lightning hit me! Six minutes left. Jesus had pulled off a major miracle! In fifty-four minutes, He had so arranged the series of events so as to open the way for me to complete what He wanted me to do. Something that normally would take many days to accomplish. I trotted down the walkway to the office door. As I walked through the door, I was stunned to see the lobby full of people. They were all standing in lines to talk to someone. There must have been a hundred or more. Every space had a line. My question would have to wait. I immediately jogged back to my car; after all, my spot was "strictly enforced."

As I was sitting in my car, thoughts flooded into my head. Jesus had done it again. It all started making sense. The restricted parking, the empty admissions office, the two empty offices where I was directed to go. Finding the education building. Catching the assistant dean "one minute" before he left for vacation. If any one of those incidents hadn't happened as it did, with the timing that was needed? *Amazing!*

Fear forgotten, I was humbled yet elated that I served such a God. A God who understands me thoroughly and knows my needs. A God who is sensitive to my fears. A God who enters into human events, and who can cause situations to come together in order to further His plans and outcomes. This particular series of events was not only to answer this reluctant sinner's mountain of prayers, but to strengthen my faith. You see, because of my fear, Jesus knew He had to demonstrate a mighty hand to overcome my weakness. He is such a wise God, who knows how to gently massage my brokenness to bring about healing.

I was emotionally drained as I drove the half hour home. I spent a few minutes in my car thanking God before going up to the condo. While attending to my mother's needs, I thought about what had just happened. I spent an anxious afternoon as I encountered the small stack of application forms. Filling them out impressed upon me that what was happening was *real*. Unless I let my fear overcome me, I was going to be a graduate student. Wow! I hadn't been in school for twelve years. I may have been in school then, but I wasn't really a student. There were perks for being a student, like discounts, cheap tickets to see music groups on campus, the student union, and inexpensive housing. The library's main use was for meeting the ladies. What would I do to compete with students younger than me who had well-developed study skills and quick minds? Then I remembered I would have a Helper who would encourage me and provide whatever I needed to fulfill His plan. I pushed myself to complete the application forms.

The next day was Wednesday. I returned to the university early in the morning, in order to turn in my admission packet and pay my application fee. I felt I needed to be prompt in completing the process so that a revival of my fears wouldn't halt the process. I knew this was a real possibility.

When I turned off the freeway, I noticed a sign as I approached the campus. I hadn't noticed it the day before. It read *PARKING GARAGE* with an arrow pointing to the right. I had passed it by one block and turned left onto the main campus. My mind raced back to the day before. *What if I had seen that sign and parked in the garage instead of parking in front of the admissions office?* The garage was on the other side of the campus from Admissions. I believe Jesus guided me to the campus parking spot in order to set off the events that transpired. Knowing my fear, He wanted to make a strong demonstration of His power in my life to help me accept what He wanted me to do. What He did was remarkable, yet I continued to doubt and to fear. He knew that, so He was persistent in demonstrating His authority over my circumstances.

I parked in the garage this time and walked quickly to the admissions building. I wondered what I would encounter. Would it be quiet, as when I first entered the day before, or crowded, like the second time? My wondering was answered as I moved toward the entry door. Several young people were going through the door as I approached. Nobody was coming out. As I entered, I realized it would be a long morning. The lines were long at each space. I asked Jesus which line I should go to. I chose one that was somewhere in the middle of the crowd. It took over an hour to move up to the front. It would have been longer, except three people gave up and left the line at various stages of the wait. They reminded me of my days at Chico State. I was highly impatient and made detrimental choices in situations like this. One time, I left a line at the bookstore when I needed a book for a very important class. When I showed up for class, somehow, eight too many students had signed up. And a couple more showed up, hoping to add the class. Students were standing along the walls. The determining factor the professor used in order to solve the overcrowding problem was who had bought the book. Several of the students left. I was one. I was my own worst enemy in those days; still am today. That's why I need Jesus!

Finally, it was my turn. I handed the young lady my packet and she looked at several pages and put check marks in various places. I guess I passed the test of filling out the application correctly. I put $40 down on the counter in anticipation of paying the application fee. She looked at me and asked a couple of questions, the last one being whether the university had received my transcripts. I told her I had only started the process the day before. She hesitated for a second, looked at the cash, and leaned forward. In a slightly lowered voice she said, "You're wasting your money.

The deadline for this semester is 5 p.m. this Friday." *Friday, 5 pm, this Friday!?* It was already Wednesday. A thought hit me: *I won't be going to school, after all.*

But somehow, I caught myself and remembered Jesus' undeniable leading the day before. He wouldn't have fashioned the timing and the divine appointments to produce yesterday's miracles, for nothing. He wouldn't have wasted His time, or mine. He *must* have a plan. I found myself blurting out to the lady, "I think God wants me to go to this school this semester." The words stunned the lady. She didn't know what to stay. I told her I wanted to pay the application fee. She accommodated me by taking my two twenty-dollar bills and giving me a receipt. I said I would try to turn in my transcripts by Friday.

She turned out to be very helpful. Unprompted, she told me that part of her responsibilities was to handle the mail that came daily. All mail had to be in her hands by 5 pm to be stamped with that day's date. She also mentioned that the university had its own mail system. All incoming mail arrived on campus at about 1 p.m. each day. It would then be sorted and delivered directly to each department. She gave me her desk number and told me to call her about 3 p.m. on Friday. I thanked her for her help and hustled back to my car, not sure what Jesus had in mind for me but, by faith, doing my best to trust in my awesome God and Savior.

10.

Official Transcript, Do Not Open

As I pulled out of the parking garage, my mind was reeling over what had just happened. Once again, Jesus had shown me how involved He is in my everyday activities. No matter the amount of bustle going on (as in the admissions office), He was able to maneuver me to the appropriate line in order for me get the information I needed. And I didn't even know what that information was! *Oxford Languages* defines the word *maneuver* as "a movement or series of moves requiring skill and care." I daresay that Jesus had demonstrated the "skill and care" to the max over the previous twenty-four hours. I am particularly drawn to the word "care" in the definition. Over the last day, Jesus showed how much He cared for me. In the midst of all the comings and goings; in the midst of my fear and reluctance, yes, Jesus showed Himself to be sovereign over everything on the campus of San Jose State University. He produced all those divine appointments with exquisite timing because He cares for me. I would die for a God like that. But the more important, and sometimes harder thing to do, is live for Him.

I was so focused on what had just happened that I don't remember much about the drive home. My mind was swirling over the goodness of God. When I got home, it was mid-morning. I immediately prayed, thanking God for His wonderful providence and asked Him for guidance in the calls that I needed to make. Then I got on the phone and called information to get the number for Chico State University (that's the way things were done in 1985). When I reached the university operator, she directed me to the admissions office. Well, here we go again, another university system. Me, needing quick help against another large, slow-moving administration. Would Jesus be up for the task? Would divine appointments and precise connections be made? It didn't take long to find out.

A lady picked up the phone on the second ring. The second ring! Not a long sequence of rings ending in a disappointing voice stating that I needed to leave a message, but a live voice, and a friendly one at that.

As I began explaining my need of having transcripts sent, she interrupted and asked if I knew that the deadline was on Friday. I answered yes and asked her if there was *any way* she could help me. All I can surmise is that the Holy Spirit prompted this lady's heart. Maybe she detected a hint of my desperation. She went into action. She took over the conversation. She told me what she was going to do and what I needed to do. I didn't have to do anything except answer her questions.

She asked me for some personal information and about which college she needed to send the transcripts to. After she had outlined what needed to happen, the lady said she was going to put down what she was currently doing and personally get my transcripts. She didn't seem concerned when I said that they were about twelve years old. She then told me what I needed to do. I needed to write a dated letter requesting the transcript be sent to San Jose State University. Included in the letter was to be a check for the fee. She asked me how many transcripts I wanted. Since I hadn't ever seen my full transcript, I asked for two. One to be sent to San Jose State, one to my home. I wondered, Would my grade point average be sufficient to qualify for enrollment? I guess I had begun to realize that graduate school might really happen, because I didn't seem to be concerned whether I would qualify. I remembered how the assistant dean had almost guaranteed admission if I got my application in. So far, I was amazed at how the call had gone. It was obvious this lady was going out of her way to help. Jesus must have sent the Holy Spirit with my call to give me favor with her. The Spirit must have been equally busy at Chico State as it was at San Jose State that morning. Their deadlines were the same. God is powerful! She confirmed my thinking when she told me it was out of the ordinary to send a transcript without a written request and fee in hand. She said that she would catch up with everything when my letter arrived. Praise God!

The next thing she said gave me pause. After getting my transcript, she would immediately prepare it for mailing. She said it would go out in a few minutes, at noon, through the US Mail. At that time, the post office was the only option. Today, my request would have been taken care of in minutes via fax. Or with an overnight delivery by Fed Ex or UPS. So, to leave my critical admission information to the US Postal Service was iffy at best. Does God have the capacity to move one letter among millions to get it where He wants? And when He wants it? The answer is obvious.

It is a mystery to me how God conducts His business amid the highways and byways of life on planet Earth. But He does. What has been mind-boggling to me is His ability to do what He does without infringing on anyone's freedom of choice. That is sacred to God. He never forces. Force is one of the adversary's main ploys. God never works that way. He is a God of love and wants His creatures to choose to follow Him on the basis of His great character. The adversary doesn't understand God's way.

The book *Patriarchs and Prophets* offers this comment, "'Why,' said the artful tempter, 'when God knew what would be the result, did He permit man to be placed on trial, to sin, and bring in misery and death?' ... There are thousands today echoing the same rebellious complaint against God. *They do not see that to deprive man of the freedom of choice would be to rob him of his prerogative as an intelligent being, and make him a mere automaton.* It is not God's purpose to coerce the will. Man was created a free moral agent" (p. 331, emphasis added).

> **He is a God of love and wants His creatures to choose to follow Him on the basis of His great character.**

This is a revealing statement about God's loving character and the freedom He offers His creatures. The adversary's claim that following God's law and way of life is restrictive, is another of his lies. God's way preserves true freedom and liberty. His law points out those things that degrade and enslave His children.

Those two ladies that morning, at their respective positions in San Jose and Chico, were not coerced to help me, or to go out of their way to give me vital assistance. God seemed to appeal to their higher nature, and they responded. They could have done otherwise. They could've "just done their job." I don't know how God does what He does, but I do know He does it with wisdom and love, without force. I am grateful He manifested His will for me that morning. And that the two ladies responded.

I thanked the lady profusely for her help. Upon ending the call, I immediately wrote the letter she requested, signed a check, and took it down to the post office for delivery. Before leaving the post office, I spent some time in my car praising and thanking God for His watchcare over me. Who am I to deserve such overwhelming manifestations of God's omnipresence? He can be wherever He needs to be. Whether San Jose or Chico. His reach is long. And He did it for a sorry sinner like me.

I spent the rest of the day helping my mother with errands and an appointment. It was relaxing to get my mind off the impending prospect of attending grad school and the fear confronting me. I needed a break from the complex activity of the previous twenty-four hours. It is amazing what Jesus can accomplish in a short time. I was so fearful and hesitant, it was only by His wonderful grace that I was able to accomplish what had transpired amid the hustle and bustle of two university campuses. It really is true that we have *nothing* to fear in this world. We have a God who is in control.

So why am I so fearful? Because the healing of my wounds, though progressing, was not complete. Which means that my faith remains incomplete. If I continue to allow Jesus to have His way with me, by His grace, I will get where He wants me to be. "Being confident of this very thing, that He who has begun a good work in you will complete *it* until the day of Jesus Christ" (Phil. 1:6). Great promise! Jesus knew that confronting those fears would further my healing. He knew that grad school would expedite that healing. The healing might ultimately be more important than the establishing a new career.

That night I attended the Wednesday night meeting at church and asked for prayer concerning my future. I needed all the prayer power that I could muster. The next morning, I awoke early to a familiar battle between faith and fear. I wrestled in bed quite a while as I prayed and dozed. Finally, I pushed myself out of bed, splashed some water on my face and went to my worship spot by the bay window. This began a Gethsemane experience that lasted most of the day. Off and on throughout the day I spent time in deep prayer.

Gethsemane was a unique and dramatic situation in Jesus' sojourn in our world. The adversary was well prepared for this onslaught in his universal controversy with Jesus. Both knew what was at stake for the human race. Jesus was burdened because He was suffering under divine justice as our Substitute and Surety. The pressure was so enormous, the Great Intercessor felt the need for His own intercessor. For the first time, He felt a tearing away from His Father. The adversary's temptations were brutal. He presented, in the starkest of terms, the uselessness of dying for the human race. The ingratitude, rejection, and the plan to kill Him, by the very people He'd come to save, was vividly portrayed before Him. Talk about love!

These temptations were greater than any human has endured. And even the Son of Man, the Creator of all, struggled with the Father's will. Under these extreme conditions, the issue that each one of us will face at some time in our walk with Jesus, was decided. Jesus fought with His human will, just as all must do. The issue was whether Jesus would *surrender His human will to His Father's will.* It was a mighty battle. Three times in the garden Jesus prayed, "not as I will, but as You *will*" (Matt. 26:39). That decision to give up His human will, in order to follow God's will, guaranteed the success of the plan of salvation, and offered us all the hope of eternal life.

Every person who calls himself or herself a follower of Jesus will have a *similar* experience at some point in their walk with Him. Of course, the stakes won't be anywhere near what Jesus encountered, but the importance for our spiritual future will be great. This is where I stood on that Thursday, waiting to see if I would be accepted into grad school.

Did I really want to do this? My fear and anxiety were great. I truly filled the description in James 1:8, "a double-minded man, unstable in all his ways." I needed to make a final choice. Even after the sensational events of the previous two days, I was wallowing in fear. The adversary presented a few arguments throughout the day as to why I shouldn't go back to school. The main argument was simply what I had always believed, that *I won't be able to do it.* Based on my academic record from my earliest days in elementary school, the evidence that I couldn't do it was overwhelming. I was a spiritual wimp as I limped through the day. I am forever grateful that God has promised *not* to tempt us beyond what we are able to withstand (see 1 Cor. 10:13).

The battle I was fighting that Thursday finally came to an end. Whether I did the right thing or not may be open for debate. I was deep in the valley of decision, the double-mindedness that James talked about. I *had* to decide. What I finally told God was this: *If the transcripts arrive on time and I am accepted, I will go back to school.* I felt I had given up my will by coming to that decision. Some say fear is a great motivator, but it can also be a great barrier, as it was in my life. But no barrier is too high if I give my will to Jesus.

Having made that decision, I calmed down and slept reasonably well that night. Upon waking, I was up and into my devotional time. Talking with Jesus had become precious to me. When He spoke back, usually through the Scriptures, I was always astonished. The Creator of the universe, the One altogether lovely, the Holy One of Israel, wanted to communicate with a sinner like me. Yes, Jesus has a strong desire to communicate with each one of His children. One of the adversary's many ploys is to distract and keep everyone busy. The noise of the world is to accomplish one thing—*muffle the voice of God.* This is why the early morning devotional time is so important. It is that time before the distractions of the world, the cell phone, the laptop, the appointment book, and the hurriedness of life snap into gear. Psalm 5:3 says, "My voice You shall hear in the morning, O LORD; In the morning I will direct *it* to You, and I will look up." On this particular morning, I had lots to talk about with Jesus. I was extra grateful for being able to speak to Him through prayer.

I tried to keep myself busy throughout the day, without much success. I had trouble keeping my eyes off the clock, as three o'clock was looming. As the time grew near, my anxiety heightened. One way to define *anxiety* is *a physical reaction to a perceived threat*. Even though I had given up my will for His will, the idea of going to graduate school seemed enormously threatening. But my mountain of prayers was about to be answered.

The direction of the next few years of my life was now hanging in the balance.

At three o'clock, I prayed one more time for God's will to be done. Breathing deeply, in an attempt to assuage my anxiety, I dialed the number that I had been given by the lady at San Jose State. It rang so long that I expected a recorded voice after each ring. No answer! I didn't know what to do. After hanging up, I did the only reasonable thing; I prayed, asking God to help me. A thought came to mind. Maybe I had dialed the wrong number. I dialed the number again, my anxiety rising. On the fourth ring someone picked up the phone, much to my delight. *It was the same lady.* I identified myself and reminded her about asking me to call at three o'clock. She remembered me and stated that the mail had been delayed and that she was in the midst of going through the stack. She said if I wanted to hold, she would finish sorting the envelopes. I wasn't going anywhere. About four or five minutes later, my heart had mixed emotions when she told me she didn't see any envelopes containing transcript from Chico State. Stunned, I asked her to take my name and number and call me if she came across the envelope.

Now what? I was dumbfounded and deflated. What's happening, Jesus? After all the miracles, divine appointments, and providential leadings at two universities, why this seemingly insurmountable hurdle? The *last* hurdle. What was the use of these blessings if I couldn't enroll? Part of me found some peace because the thought occurred that I wouldn't have to go to school. In the recent past, that would have been a cause to celebrate, but now it was greatly diminished. I was overwhelmed by the change in circumstances after so many providential leadings. What did all of this mean?

I went to my devotional spot and plopped down in the chair. I didn't really pray, I just sat there and looked out the window. After a few uncomfortable minutes, a thought came. *Wait on the Lord.* I knew that verse well and looked it up. "Wait on the Lord; be of good courage, and He shall strengthen your heart; wait, I say, on the LORD!" (Ps. 27:14). After a couple of years of Jesus' working on my impatience, He had changed me enough so that I didn't get totally out of control when things didn't go my way. Though I still had miles to go, some progress had been made in this area. I chose to accept the situation and let Jesus work things out. I had thoughts about the office lady calling and saying she had found the letter. Also, I thought that maybe all that had happened over the last few days was to get me enrolled, ultimately, for the next semester. Knowing my fear, maybe He was going to give me some time to adjust as I waited for the next semester. My mind was churning. What did I know? All I knew was that God doesn't make mistakes. He knows exactly what He is doing in every situation, even this one.

I was awakened from my thoughts by my mother asking if I had picked up the mail. She was waiting for a check to arrive. I got up and walked down the flight of stairs to the bank of mailboxes. After using my key to open the box, I grabbed a small handful of mail. As I began walking up the stairs, I quickly scanned through the mail. To my utter shock, there was a letter from Chico State. I turned it over to read *OFFICIAL TRANSCRIPT, DO NOT OPEN* stamped where the letter had been sealed. Endorphins were popping in my brain! I broke out laughing in the stairwell. I was overwhelmed. Not because the final hurdle was removed. No. Because I serve such a mighty God.

I had forgotten that I had requested two sets of transcripts from Chico State, one to be sent to my home. In my excitement, I looked at my watch and noted that it was three forty. I sobered up quickly as I realized I had only a little time to deliver the letter before the five o'clock deadline. I ran up the last few steps and hurriedly grabbed my shoes, told my mother I had to go to San Jose, and headed to the garage. Once I entered the freeway, I noticed the rush hour traffic was beginning to form. This could be a game changer. But the traffic kept moving at a fair pace as I made the half-hour drive to San Jose State. I must have hit the very beginning of what would be stop-and-go for the next few hours on a Friday afternoon. I spent that half hour reviewing what had happened since three o'clock. I wondered if Jesus set circumstances in motion, to work out as they did, in order to give me even more evidence that He was in control of the situation. I guess He knew I needed more help in the faith area. What a gentle God.

When I made it to the university, I headed directly to the parking garage. Having parked, I noticed there weren't as many cars as the last time I was there. I wondered if that would mean the admissions office would be less crowded. That would be a blessing. As I jogged across the campus, I noticed there weren't as many people around. I also wondered if simply being in line before five o'clock I would be served, even if it was after five. My anxiety festered as my first question was answered as I entered the building. It was busy, but not quite as busy as the last time. I prayed again for Jesus to lead me to the correct line. I decided to go to the shortest line. I didn't find an answer to my second question. The person in front of me didn't know if we would be served after five o'clock, either.

I had arrived on campus at four-twenty. It took another five minutes to jog across campus. So I was in line by four twenty-five. Would thirty-five minutes be enough? There I was, waiting again. You would think, with all that had happened over the last three days, that I would be at peace with what was happening. But I wasn't. Though I'm sure those around me didn't notice anything out of the ordinary with my demeanor, I was struggling inside. My negative emotions were raging. Cognitively I had made a decision to trust Jesus. Yet I was a basket case. My damaged emotions hadn't caught up with my cognitive functions yet. Fortunately, faith is based on choice not emotions. So I waited.

As my line shortened, I was able to get a glimpse at what was being transacted at the counter. I saw a couple of people give cash or a check to the lady. I suddenly realized I hadn't brought any money for tuition! In fact, I didn't even know how much tuition was. Well, I rationalized that I would have plenty of time to pay the following week. I had already paid the application fee. I just needed to submit the transcript before five o'clock. At least that's what I thought needed to happen. I would turn in the transcript and come back sometime the following week to pay the tuition. That was somehow comforting as the line continued to shorten. Finally, there were only two people in front of me.

It was now four forty-five. I was hopeful that I would make the deadline. Surprisingly, the two were together and only needed to make some kind of payment. Their transaction went quickly. There I was, facing the young lady at about four-fifty. Jesus comes through again! I informed her of why I was there and handed her the coveted transcript.

What a satisfying end to the last four days. The lady took the envelope and, upon checking the stamp on the back, added her own stamp with the time and date and set it aside with some other envelopes. I didn't give her any details, but I said, "That envelope is a miracle." I wanted to move along because there were a couple of people behind me, so I quickly asked her about the tuition. She told me the amount (a pittance by today's standard). I thanked her and said I would be back sometime the following week to pay it. What she replied sent shock waves down my spine. She said, "You will have to pay it on Monday, classes begin on Tuesday."

Tuesday! You've got to be kidding! That's only four days away. I left the building with my mind spinning and that familiar fear and anxiety returned. Jesus, when will this turmoil ever end? Will I ever have some peace about these events? *Tuesday.*

For some reason, I flashed back to my experience at Chico State. Here it was, five o'clock on Friday, and I knew the education department would be closed. The bookstore would be closed. Yikes, that reminded me that I didn't even have a class schedule to know what books to purchase. I didn't even know which classroom to go to on Tuesday. I longed for peace, even a little. Once

> *Sitting in my car, I prayed for some relief from the turmoil. I thanked Jesus for all He was doing for me in answer to my mountain of prayers. I also confessed my lack of faith in the face of insurmountable evidence of His grace.*

again, you would think after all that had transpired, starting at camp meeting, that I would have peace. Even when this latest curveball caught me off guard. But I didn't. I was a jumble of emotions. The wounds I carried from my past experiences with formal education were raising their ugly heads. I started walking briskly back to the parking garage, taking deep breaths in hope of minimizing my anxiety. Sitting in my car, I prayed for some relief from the turmoil. I thanked Jesus for all He was doing for me in answer to my mountain of prayers. I also confessed my lack of faith in the face of insurmountable evidence of His grace. This time of prayer was beneficial in realigning faith over feelings—something that we all need to do.

On the way home, I battled the bumper-to-bumper traffic. I decided on a plan of action for Monday. I was regaining my emotional footing by taking some positive steps toward dealing with the problem. Or, at least, the problem as I perceived it. Jesus already knew what was going to happen. If I'd had more faith at the time, I would have enjoyed the weekend more. Instead, I spent most of the weekend asking God to bless my simple plan. Much of the plan hinged on the assistant dean's remarks earlier in the week suggesting that, if I completed the application process, he would "get me in." So I would call him early Monday morning and apprise him of my progress and ask him what I should be doing the rest of the day. Settling on a plan was most helpful. It enabled me to see a way forward and be able to leave it in God's hands for the weekend. Mostly.

On Monday I was up early as usual, for devotions. I had much to praise God for. Even if He hadn't manifested such a strong hand for me last week, He deserved all the honor and glory and praise that I could muster. "I will praise you, O Lord my God, with all my heart, and I will glorify your name forevermore. For great *is* Your mercy toward me, and You have delivered my soul from the depths of Sheol" (Ps. 86:12, 13). Unfortunately, for me, when something significant is happening in my life, it infringes on my devotional time and interferes with my communion with God. Yes, important things should be a part of worship, but when they repeatedly invade praise, confession, Scripture reading, thanksgiving, or intercession, it is quite disturbing. Sadly, I have a major struggle with distractibility during worship. I look forward to that time when I will physically praise God in the heavenly sanctuary with those "ten thousand times ten thousand, and thousands of thousands" of angels (see Rev. 5:11). In the presence of God and the Lamb there will be no distractions.

After my devotions, I moved forward with my plan for the day by calling the assistant dean to give him an update on my progress in enrolling. Then I would ask what I needed to do to start classes the next day. The *next* day! Even though this happened thirty-five years ago, as I just wrote the words *next day,* I experienced a twinge of anxiety. It remains unbelievable to me what Jesus had done in answering my mountain of prayers. And the way He went about doing it. I must have needed the series of undeniable miracles because of my fear, anxiety, and reluctance. He demonstrated His power in such a way, probably, because it was the only way to reach me.

So I made the call fairly early and had to leave a message. I assumed he would be back from vacation and in his office, preparing for the semester. If I didn't receive a call back by noon, I would drive down to the university and talk with the department secretary. Either way, I needed to pay the tuition in order to complete the process. While waiting for the call, I took care of my responsibilities around the condo, got dressed, and set out breakfast for my mother. I wanted to be ready when the call came so I could leave immediately. Within the hour, the call came. I thanked him for returning my call and briefly explained what had transpired since we had talked. He commended me for my diligence. If only he knew.

Of course, the first thing he suggested was paying the tuition. He also promised to call the admissions office and make sure everything was completed on their end. I asked him about a class schedule. In the midst of the previous whirlwind week, I hadn't even thought about what classes I would take. I knew nothing about the program, except that Jesus wanted me involved. His response was, "Don't worry about those things now." He went on to say that all I needed to do was show up at a certain classroom at four o'clock the next day for orientation. Then we would get together later in the week and determine what program emphasis I was interested in pursuing. He also informed me that classes met on Tuesdays and Thursdays at four o'clock. Thus, I was introduced to the laissez-fare structure of the program. Having never been in grad school, I didn't know what to expect. As the program played out, I discovered there was a lack of structure in many of the classes, which had been purposely built into the program in order to facilitate stirring up personal issues. But I'm getting ahead of myself.

After the call, I immediately left for the university. Based on everything that had happened over the last few days, I wondered what Jesus had in store for this visit. Upon arrival, I went to the admission office and paid the semester tuition. A lofty amount of $375! I couldn't believe it. I was officially a student at San Jose State University. What a journey! For the first time, my being in that building lacked the overwhelming anxiety of the previous visits. That's not to say there wasn't some emotional turmoil, however.

Being in this new situation, this new environment, with unknown challenges ahead, was disconcerting. My insecurities were still rampant. *What am I doing here? How am I going to do grad school-level work?* Once again, I was reminded that I wasn't going to be doing this alone. Jesus would be with me. *Hadn't He clearly demonstrated that this was where I was supposed to be? Hadn't He shown that He was more than up to the task? That He knew what He was doing? Didn't I have a promise to claim?* The answer was yes to each question. A promise was given to Joshua thousands of years ago when He was called to the enormous task of taking over for Moses in leading the Israelites. He faced many unknown challenges. He must have been strengthened for the task when he heard the words "I will not leave you nor forsake you" (Josh. 1:5). Was I going to believe that promise? Had Jesus not shown that He was with me? *Oh, how my weaknesses plague me.*

Next, I took a mini tour of the campus. I went to the bookstore, the library, the student union, and the athletic center. It was strange to be on a university campus after so many years. I wondered how long it would take to feel comfortable and a part of the scene. After lunch I returned home. When I arrived back at my car, it dawned on me that this was my first visit to the campus when something spectacular hadn't happened. Some manifestation of God's glory. That realization brought a sense of humility, a deep gratefulness for what Jesus had done for me over a few days that August in 1985.

When I got home, I brought my mother up to speed about the changes that were coming to the routine we had developed over time. She was very supportive and interested in what was happening. When I talked with the assistant dean, it sounded as if I didn't have to do anything in preparation for the following day. I just needed to show up. So I spent the evening reading and doing the usual chores. My anxiety was ebbing as I perceived little threat concerning Tuesday.

The next day was a different story, as the reality of what had miraculously happened the previous week came to the forefront of my mind. For the first time in many years, I was actually going to be sitting in a classroom. Driving to class that day was difficult; my anxiety was rising as the miles passed by. Upon arriving at the parking garage, I had some time to pray, asking Jesus for peace. It didn't help much. The education department was on the same side of campus as the parking garage, so it was a short walk to class. I was one of the early arrivals and found myself sitting there with hot flashes and cold sweats. I was miserable and afraid.

I didn't *choose* these emotions; they just rose up from the very depths of my soul, where sin resides. Sin is more than rebellious choices and disobedience. Sin is also a condition that comes, unfortunately, from being created in this world. It's unavoidable. It's that brokenness, which results from being born with a deformed, selfish core. Then, as we sojourn through this world, we are further wounded by the arrows of the adversary. Praise God for the promise of healing through the death of His Son. As I sat there waiting for orientation to begin, I was vulnerable because of my wounds and weaknesses; they were exacerbated in this educational setting, because it was far from my comfort zone. Yet God was going to use this setting to further the healing of those wounds—and to reveal the "big lie" in my life.

11.

The Big Lie

The Red Sea incident in Exodus 14 was a demonstration of God's mercy to a band of people who knew little about Him. It was an attempt not only to deliver His people out of bondage, but also to re-ignite their faith. After 400 years of slavery in Egypt, the Israelites had mostly lost the knowledge of God. Faith was at a premium. The Red Sea account is one of a multitude of Old Testament stories that reveal the gospel of deliverance from the slavery of sin. God knew that He needed to do something impressive to get their attention, something to reveal His mighty power to deliver, something to let the Israelites know with whom they were dealing. You would have thought that one of the greatest physical manifestations of God's ability, revealed in Scripture, would quickly establish the Israelites' faith. Unfortunately, faith is not easily established. I can attest to that. In this fantastic incident, God demonstrated His great love, concern, and watchcare over His people. Sadly, it was only a few weeks later that the Israelites constructed the golden calf.

Jesus knew that I was no different from the Israelites. He knew that I needed a powerful demonstration of His love for me and His ability to handle my life. He knew that my fear of education would be a deterrent to my following His lead. So He set up a personal Red Sea experience to help strengthen my faith and answer my mountain of prayers. With Pharaoh's army bearing down on the Israelites, they mustered enough faith (or maybe fear) to heed Moses' call to cross the sea and proceed onto dry ground. With all that Jesus had done for me since camp meeting, especially during the last few days, I would have been a fool not to have entered the dry ground. The walls of water were ferocious, the advancing army of fears were in pursuit. What could I do but follow where Jesus had opened a way? It may not always be easy to follow His way, but it is the safest.

So there I sat, with hot flashes and cold sweats, waiting for the orientation to begin. My emotions were at a stretch, my anxiety at a high point. *What am I doing here?* As the class started filling up, I was surprised to see that most of the students were about my age. I soon found out that they were mostly veteran teachers who were wanting to add a counseling certificate to their resume, or looking for new job opportunities. The dean and his assistant, the one who had helped me, got things started by initiating what is called a social mixer. People identified themselves and shared their goals for being in the program. With dry mouth, I minimally shared and stated that I wasn't sure what I wanted from the program. The assistant dean, smiling, remarked that it would be taken care of tomorrow. I was comforted by his remark. He ended up being an encouragement and a resource for me throughout the program.

We met the following day in his office. He wanted to know about my background and goals. As we looked at alternatives and objectives, it became clear that counseling in an educational setting was not the way for me to go. Because I knew so little about the program and the different tracks I could follow, I was praying for Jesus to manifest His plan. When the track for marriage and family counseling was presented, I immediately knew that was for me. Many of my divine appointments in the past had involved marriage or family. He gave me the curriculum, and we put together the first semester's class schedule, which were introductory. As our time drew to a close, I thanked him for his help and for his encouraging words at the orientation. I was embarrassed when He told me that he knew I was struggling with fear. Was it that obvious? As it turned out, he was quite insightful, as a good counselor should be.

I left there and went directly to the bookstore. As I crossed campus I wondered if there would be any books left. Surely all the used books would be gone at this late date. I was able to buy only one used book; the rest were new, at a premium price. Textbooks and I have had a long painful history of not getting along. I was a slow, methodical reader with poor recall. After a couple of weeks, I was grossly behind. I found out that the education department had a reading laboratory, and I could engage in some testing. The testing revealed nothing new. My reading was barely average, but the recall was inadequate. I would have to rely on Jesus for help in this area.

In each class, which lasted roughly ninety minutes, I felt overwhelmed, out of my league. I was so wounded and rusty with regard to school that everything was too much for me. It was all I could do to make it through a class. I was afraid of being discovered for who I knew I was. A fraud, a fake, who was over his head in these classes. I was fearful because being discovered would lead to shame. Not guilt—*shame.* Guilt means I did something wrong. I stole the candy bar. Shame is in a whole different realm. Shame means I am wrong; my whole being is wrong. The difference between the two is immense, almost unbridgeable. This struggle caused me to be very protective of what I said and did. And this was before any tests or papers were required. I was struggling to keep Jesus and the Bible promise, which I had always claimed, before me.

In one class, I was challenged immediately. Right from the start, they wanted us to begin experiencing the process of being a counselor and a client. This was one of the classes that was structured to "stir up your stuff." I didn't need much help in that department! We broke up into small groups of about six students each. We were led by a second-year student who assisted the professor. First, we would meet in the small group. We were introduced to some basic group counseling concepts. We would interact with each other around a suggested topic. In the first group, I was astonished when the leader suggested the first topic. "Share with the group what is your greatest fear." Wow! On the one hand, here was a topic I could readily talk about. On the other hand, this was our first meeting. Who were these people? Could they be trusted with my "stuff"? Confidentiality had been explained as a bedrock of the counseling process. *What is said in group, stays in group.* When it came to my turn, I hesitantly informed the group of my situation. And I closed with a direct statement that my greatest fear was that I wasn't going to be able to do the work. *I never had before, and so why would I now?* I was surprised that I was so verbal. I guess it needed to come out.

Then the leader asked us to pick a partner for one-on-one peer counseling. I was paired up with a forty-something lady teacher. We would be working together for the semester. First one of us would be the counselor, then we would trade places. The time always passed quickly. Neither of us knew what we were doing. I don't know if Jesus was prompting her, but she was direct and challenging. She wouldn't let me off with the statement that I wasn't going to be able to do the work. When I was the client, this was the focus of our sessions. I would frustrate her with my excuses and diversions. Wounds heal best when they are tended to in a positive way. I had the Master Physician working on mine. But they were deep and had festered a long, long time. Beginning to face these inadequacies head-on was difficult and challenging, but therapeutic in the long run. Jesus was using this lady and many assignments and situations, as school progressed, to bring about the healing that I needed. The program turned out to be a rehabilitation hospital for me. At the end of that first semester, I had to admit to the group that I was having to revisit my previous statement at the beginning of the semester. I was surprising myself with excellent grades!

Though quietly pleased, I knew that this semester's work was fear driven. I was doing everything out of fear. I would arrive at the campus an hour before class. I would complete my assignments two weeks early. I would spend long hours studying. All good learning habits, but fueled by fear. Though doing well, I was afraid of not being able to maintain my success. I never had before. And fear-based success was a drag on the emotions. There was little satisfaction, but Jesus was teaching me some things. I was beginning to see a glimpse of "the big lie" that I believed.

The big lie? It is a hindrance, a burden every person unknowingly has to deal with, in one degree or another. The big lie is a set of false beliefs, false understandings about ourselves, which are the result of living in a fallen world. Over time, through family communication and detrimental life events, these falsehoods shape what we believe about ourselves; they create our self-image, often exceedingly distorted. And this leads to making life choices based on the lies that we believe about ourselves.

As I mentioned before, the adversary has a PhD in the human family. To be concise, he watches what happens in the family and notices the weak points of the family system. Unfortunately, because of sin, all families have weaknesses. Some more than others. Mistakes are made, regrettable teachings are unknowingly passed down from parents to children. Detrimental messages, spoken and unspoken, pass from generation to generation. Parents disoriented from substance abuse, do hurtful, selfish acts. Not to mention the unspeakable exploitation and trauma that occur in all too many families. The family system is one of the strongest forces in the world for shaping belief and behavior.

In the family system, there is a grave truth. A child is like a sponge, soaking up their environment. Whatever the child observes and is taught in the family invades his or her sensitive psychological and emotional systems. Then, when the child leaves the home, the teachings, world view, "family wisdom," and wounds from mistreatment and mistakes, accompany the child. The adversary has observed these dysfunctions and makes sure situations happen in the broader experience of life that further cement the falsehoods in the growing young adults' self-understanding. Unfortunately, this is a reality for each family. The only hope, as with everything in life, is Jesus, the fountain of truth. Powerfully mixed in with the disruptions of the adversary can be the life-giving teachings of the

Bible and the working of the Holy Spirit. Regrettably, most families are unwilling or unable to access the vitalizing principles of Scripture.

This earthly family situation seems unfair. But it is a reality of life. The second of the Ten Commandments (see Exod. 20:5) presents this principle, which is known in family studies as the *generational transmission process*. Though it is presented in the context of idol worship, the principle seems the same, and the application to the family rings true. Through hereditary tendencies, sinful choices, and cultural values, the dysfunction and false beliefs are passed down from parent to child. Surely Jesus weeps as He sees so many families hurting.

A prime example is my family. Because of my parents' situation of growing up during the Great Depression, education was not a priority. Survival was. So when I came along there was little, if any, value placed on learning. Along with my distractibility and my elementary-school experience, and the years of struggle with school failure as a young adult, my big lie was established. What was that lie? That I was a non-learner. I wasn't an achiever. I was merely to get by in life. In Jesus' wisdom, it was now time to begin healing the wound that caused the lie. Praise God.

The peer-counseling class wasn't the only class that first semester to "stir up my stuff." Every class was keeping my *stuff* at high tide. It seemed that some of the classes were left open ended, and I found that disconcerting. I needed direction, boundaries, and structure. But, somehow, I survived—even flourished. I give all the glory to God and the promise I claimed daily throughout the semester, "I can do all things through Christ who strengthens me" (Phil. 4:13). It was a safeguard in the many times when my anxiety would threaten to undo me. Jesus is so faithful. It seemed He reserved one class every semester to particularly stir the pot. That particular class would threaten me each semester. The anxiety would be overwhelming on the day of the class. A required class in statistics almost put me in the hospital. For classes like that I would claim an additional promise, "And my God shall supply all your need according to His riches in glory by Christ Jesus" (Phil. 4:19). And then hang on for dear life.

Something tremendous happened at the library. It was my first written assignment. I wasn't as overwhelmed by this assignment because we could choose our own topic. I chose *divorce*. I needed ten references. It was the library itself that caused me to break into a sweat. San Jose State is located in Silicon Valley, and in 1985, it was showered with the latest technology from the rising tech giants. At the time, I had never touched a computer, let alone know what a mouse was. So I was afraid as I walked across campus, claiming promises as I went. I remember clearly the agony, the fear, and the anxiety as I walked through the entrance. But I also remembered Jesus and took a deep breath as I entered the lobby. There was a crowd of students waiting for the elevator. I estimated there were at least enough students to fill the elevator three times before I could get on.

Because I was almost paralyzed anyway, it was easy to just stand and wait. I moved over to some waist-high shelves and set my briefcase down on top. As God is my witness, this is what happened over the next hour. I didn't know it, but the shelf I was leaning on was the outer part of the reference section of the library. I recognized the long, narrow catalog drawers and the large reference catalogs. I was familiar with how they worked, but strangely, there was no one using them. As I stood there, I bumped my briefcase and it fell off the shelf. As I picked it up, there was a reference catalog lying open. The briefcase had been on top of it. As I looked down my eye fell on the top of the alphabetized list on the page. It read *Divorce*. I couldn't believe my eyes. I trembled and went down the column while waiting for the elevator. By the time the crowd had thinned out and I could access the elevator, I had three solid references to look up. I went upstairs and stumbled around a little before finding the section I needed. I somehow found the two articles and the book listed in the reference catalog. I found five more references from the footnotes in the articles and the book, for a total of eight references. I knew I could easily pick up two or more. In about an hour and a half, by God's grace, I had found everything I needed.

What did I learn from this incident? Aside from learning about the factors that lead to divorce, I learned that Jesus knows every page of every book and article in the San Jose State library. And He knows how to get me to them. The implications of such power are unfathomable. It led to more questions and observations about the power of the Holy Spirit to work out the events that needed to take place: My timing to arrive at the library when it was so crowded that I had to wait; the reference catalog lying open to the very page I needed; the factors involved to have someone leave the catalog open to that particular page. These things don't happen by chance. The great God of the universe oversees all these things, and an infinite number more. No detail is too insignificant for His attention. He demonstrated once again that He cared for me and that I had nothing to worry about. What looks so complex to us is just another day at the office for the Godhead. I have an ever-growing list of questions about such incidents to ask Jesus when I see Him face to face.

A little devotional book entitled *Steps to Christ* summarizes God's watchcare over all the affairs of life, big and small. To believe this means increased peace.

> Keep your wants, your joys, your sorrows, your cares, and your fears before God. You cannot burden Him; you cannot weary Him. He who numbers the hairs of your head is not indifferent to the wants of His children. "The Lord is very pitiful, and of tender mercy." (James 5:11). His heart of love is touched by our sorrows and even by our utterances of them. Take to Him *everything* that perplexes the mind. Nothing is too great for Him to bear, for He holds up worlds, He rules over all the affairs of the universe. *Nothing that in any way concerns our peace is too small for Him to notice.* There is no chapter in our experience too dark for Him to read; there is no perplexity too difficult for Him to unravel. No calamity can befall the least of His children, no anxiety harass the soul, no joy cheer, no sincere prayer escape the lips, of *which our heavenly Father is unobservant, or in which He takes no immediate interest.* "He healeth the broken in heart, and bindeth up their wounds." Psalm 147:3. The relations between God and each soul are as distinct and full as though there were not another soul upon the earth to share His watchcare, not another soul for whom He gave His beloved Son. (White, p. 100, emphasis added)

Wow! I can trust a God like that. I needed a God like that as I navigated places like the library and investigated information in classes that overwhelmed me.

Though I was doing well, my fear and distrust of my abilities led to a couple of decisions. First, the program was designed to be completed in two years. I decided to take fewer classes each semester in order to reduce my anxiety. I worked it out so that my last semester would be composed solely of completing my master's thesis, without any other responsibilities. This seemed to be the best thing for my well-being and my grades. I would then take three years to complete the program. I was okay with that.

The second decision was influenced by impatience more than fear. In a conversation with another student, I found out that, after someone completed a master's program in marriage and family counseling, the State of California required 3,000 hours of supervised internship. Upon completing the hours, an intern would then qualify to take a written test. If you failed the test, then you would have to wait six months to retake it. If you passed, you would spend the next six months preparing for an oral exam. Once again, a failure would cause another six-month delay before retaking the exam. This information was not what I wanted to hear. Even if everything went my way after San Jose State, it would be at least three more years to acquire my license. That would total six years. I couldn't accept that. I would be more than forty years old at the end of it all.

I was shaken up by this information. In my impatience, the future looked extremely distant. I prayed about it, but I wasn't being honest with myself, or with Jesus. So I went to my advisor and, after discussing my concerns, decided to change the emphasis in my program. I switched to a program in which I would learn to help people make career transitions in their lives. I thought my business background would be helpful. This was *my* decision; I had to live with it. It was *my* choice, which I had a right to make. God always gives us that right. Of course, the repercussions of my choice are mine to deal with; that's always the case.

> *If I am willing, Jesus will eventually get me where He wants me to be. And I will learn valuable lessons along the way.*

It is comforting to realize that Jesus is never caught off guard by the things we do. He is the "Alpha and the Omega, *the* Beginning and *the* End" (Rev. 1:8). This means that Jesus is in full control of the past, the present, and the future. He knew that I would make this decision long before I had made it. How all this works in the heavenly realm is beyond me, but we can be secure in His love and wisdom. If I am willing, Jesus will eventually get me where He wants me to be. And I will learn valuable lessons along the way. At the time, this decision reduced some of my anxiety and enabled me to move forward in my studies more easily.

I made it through the first semester. There was some satisfaction, but not much peace. I felt that I couldn't relax; that I had to be on guard against slipping back into old, dysfunctional study habits. Just before the second semester started, I paid my tuition. This left me with little money. I began praying about the situation. There was a semester and summer break for God to provide. "And my God shall supply" kept coming to mind (Phil. 4:19). The semester started and I was ready for the grind. I had that one class that God chose to use to "stir up my stuff." It is very important for counselors to have an understanding of their "stuff"; that is, their own weaknesses and issues. You know, stuff. This knowledge minimizes any interference the weakness may cause in the counseling relationship. Thus, revealing my weaknesses was a necessity if I was going to be beneficial to others. And no doubt a big blessing for me. As rough as it was, I knew it was helping my healing and growth. Jesus certainly knows what He is doing. I did well that semester and looked forward to the summer.

I had one setback, on the financial front. I saw a flyer about student loans, and about halfway through the semester I decided to apply. I had taken loans at Chico State and paid them off years before. Back then, loans to students weren't the burden that they are today. By applying, I was basically giving God an opportunity, an avenue to provide for my needs. I had also applied for a job at the library but was told there were no openings. I was using the principle of seeking and finding, knocking and the door being opened (see Matt 7:7–8). I was searching, looking for God's provision.

I was stunned when I picked up the application at the financial office. It was thirty-eight pages long! I do not like filling out forms like that. They frustrate me. It asked many questions that weren't on the application years before. I hurriedly filled it out and returned it. I asked the lady at the desk why they asked so many questions. She replied that the change was caused by the upsurge of fraud in the student-loan industry, which had occurred in the last few years. Made perfect sense.

About two weeks later, I received a rejection letter. The reason for being turned down was that since I lived with my mother, I didn't meet the criteria for qualifying. I thought there might be some mistake, so I asked for an appointment with one of the financial counselors. The counselor told me that the computer had lumped me in with teenagers who were still living with their parents. I explained that I was in my mid-thirties, had owned my own house, been married, and was taking care of my mother. She was understanding and sympathetic, but said that the computer didn't take that type of information into account. So that door was closed and my bank account continued to dwindle. Jesus must have another way.

Heading into finals, I saw that nothing had changed with my financial status. So I decided to look for any job as soon as finals were over. I started a job with a temp agency a couple of days after finals ended. Along with many other students, I began cleaning the dormitories at Stanford University. My height made it a back-breaking job, but it was work. And it wouldn't be forever. The job lasted for just a few weeks, and I earned enough to cover tuition, books, gas, and sundry items for the upcoming semester. God was faithful and provided for all my needs.

In late summer, my third semester began. That statistics class was on my schedule. I knew it was going to be a rough few months. It was completely over my head. Numbers, collecting, and analyzing and interpreting data was not my forte. It was as if I had no insight at all. I survived the class, even receiving a grade I didn't think I had earned. The rest of my classes were going well, even though I still struggled with anxiety. I was, however, fitting in more, contributing more, and enjoying my classmates. Near the end of the semester my financial situation was still shaky. I had to focus some time and energy on finding God's provision. About a week later, I received a letter in the mail. It was from some foundation I didn't recognize. Wow! It said they were going to pay my expenses for the next semester. I called the financial office to find out if they had any information. The young lady I talked with sounded like a student; she didn't seem to know much about it. I thanked the Lord and went back to my studies with one less burden.

A week or two later, I received another letter in the mail. It was from the same foundation. The news in this communication was even better than that in the first letter. They informed me that they were awarding me a perpetual scholarship as long as I was in school—*all expenses paid!* I was stunned. I had earned a scholarship? Me? Come on! I set up an appointment with the financial counselor to find out how this could have happened. I showed her the letter. She told me it was a private foundation in Sacramento. I asked her how they got my name. She asked me if I remembered filling out one of the pages in the application that pertained to scholarships. I didn't remember that at all. I was frustrated and impatient when I filled out that lengthy application. Isn't Jesus something?

Jesus didn't stop there; a few days later the university library called and offered me a fifteen-hour a week job. I ask the man if I could call him right back. With my sudden scholarship, I wondered if I needed a job that would take a fifteen-hour bite out of my study time. I talked to Jesus about the situation. I called the man back and accepted the job. It turned out to be the perfect job. It entailed being a clerk in the reference library. The reference library was located in the "old" library, which was tucked away behind some newer buildings. At this library, books checked out could be used only on the premises. Usually only a handful of students would come in on my shift. This led to much study time for me. I also used a computer for the first time, in order to check the books in and out. I must have done a good job because they hired me full-time for the summer. I must emphasize again; all of these blessings weren't happenstance. They came directly from the Creator of the universe. He who created the sun, moon, and stars and keeps them working in perfect sync, is interested in my little life. Magnificent God!

Near the end of the second semester, I decided to take a weekend off to attend an Adventist singles campout. It was an annual event held in Yosemite National Park, one of my favorite places. I hadn't attended a singles event since the international conference at Pacific Union College, where I learned so much about healing from divorce. This was a popular national event, so there were hundreds of people from all over the USA attending. It was more of a social event than the intensive conference I attended before. I liked that. I needed some casual down time, and you couldn't have picked a better place for that than Yosemite. There were the usual devotionals, walking, bike riding, hiking, social events, food, and a nightly speaker. For the most part, I was able to disengage from the anxiety of school and enjoy myself.

On the last night, my tentmate informed me that he had invited a young lady to come to our tent for some hot chocolate. When she showed up, she had a friend with her, an attractive Japanese woman named Carolyn and that balanced things socially. We had interesting time together. My tentmate was funny and entertaining and kept the conversation at a high pitch. After a while, he went for a walk with his new friend. That left me with the lovely Carolyn. After attending the Japanese church for a while, I had become appreciative of Asian beauty. As we talked, I mentioned my current situation at San Jose State and the pressure I felt. She said she could relate, as she had recently completed studies at Loma Linda School of Medicine.

We didn't talk all that long. I found out that she was in a long-term relationship that she recently decided was quickly eroding. I also had a friend I would spend time with when I could. I told her about my membership at the Mountain View Japanese Church. She mentioned she had visited there many times because her aunt and uncle were members. I laughed when she told me their name. They were my best friends at the church! The following day the camp ended, and we went our separate ways. Of course, her relatives in Mountain View had nothing but rave reviews about her when I told them we had met.

I was back to the grind. Still doing better than I ever hoped, but still struggling with my weaknesses. One of the things that worked in my favor was that there weren't very many exams. As I mentioned earlier, the program was very different from anything I had been involved with in the past. Instead of exams, the emphasis was on written papers, oral presentations, and group collaborations, along with practical applications such as the peer-counseling class. This reduced my anxiety, as I always struggled with exams the most.

I think it would be fair to categorize the program as "New Age." It was the 1980s, and the New Age movement had captured the imagination of educators, especially on the West Coast. Santa Cruz was about thirty-five miles over the hill from San Jose. Santa Cruz was a mecca for New Age thinking. At least half of the people in the program were from Santa Cruz. They were highly influenced by what was going on there. The majority of professors were of the same mindset. So what was a fairly conservative Seventh-day Adventist doing, attending a secular college that is swayed by this anti-Biblical world view?

The easy answer is that Jesus placed me in the program. As the miraculous admission events unrolled, I had never given a thought to the kind of program or the teachings I would be introduced to. Even if I did have thoughts, it wouldn't have mattered. The God of heaven made it abundantly clear, didn't He? The Red Sea had opened wide. It was the only path I could take. I would have been a complete fool to do otherwise. If Jesus leads you somewhere, then His protection will be involved in everything you do. He never sends someone without preparing the way.

> *So what was a fairly conservative Seventh-day Adventist doing, attending a secular college that is swayed by this anti-Biblical world view?*

Take the Old Testament stories of Joseph and Daniel or Paul in the New Testament. I never had the privilege of attending a Christian school, so this wasn't a big deal for me. But the bottom line was that Jesus said Go! Were some aberrant subjects taught? Yes. An example is Neuro-linguistic programming (NLP). Developed in the 1970s by two men named Bandler and Grinder, it was one of the topics in a class. It is a pseudoscientific approach to, among other things, psychotherapy. I remember it because in one class, I saw a video that was shot in a packed gymnasium at the University of California, Santa Cruz. I was taken aback by what I saw. Two people, separately, were interviewed by Bandler concerning issues they were dealing with. In just a few minutes, with Bandler identifying the *root* of their problems, he "delivered" them. The classroom was speechless while the video played. Quite a discussion followed; I didn't participate.

I thought it was the work of the adversary of our souls. But if you're where Jesus wants you to be, you will have all the protection you need.

A course in *dreams* was coming up on my schedule later in my program. After talking to another student about it, I didn't want to spend my time in that class. So I started praying. When the semester came around, I resigned myself to having to take the course. The day before the class started, there was an announcement that a second section of that class was going to be offered. I was surprised and thankful for another answered prayer. I submitted a request to change classes. When I showed up on the first day, six other students were there. I was pleased as the new teacher explained the focus of the class: concrete issues for counselors, as opposed to something as abstract and as esoteric as dreams. The next week, when we met again, there were only three students. The professor went ahead and started the class. We continued to meet the following week with three students. I was in the department secretary's office one day and somehow our conversation drifted to the new class. She made the comment that she couldn't understand why that class was still meeting. There had to be a minimum of six students enrolled to validate a class. I knew why.

A major principle of counseling is that every person's beliefs should be accepted. A client's belief system (no matter how destructive) gives some evidence of where they are in their life. Part of the counselor's work is to help facilitate a positive change in the client's life. So in a program like the one at San Jose State, acceptance of other student's beliefs provided an opportunity for understanding your own biases and prejudices.

Everybody's got them, biases and prejudices. This led to many open discussions on various philosophies and world views in class. My view on Biblical Christianity was in the minority, to say the least, but there were others out of the mainstream, as well. Early on, I was fairly quiet in these discussions because of my struggles. It was difficult to speak up when I was so unsure of myself.

Later in the program, I felt more confident in speaking up. I did have a few opportunities for witnessing with individual classmates. The one opportunity to witness that comes clearly to mind was in a small-group roundtable discussion. Jesus showed up, big time. People were openly sharing their beliefs. There was quite a variety. The lady just before me was talking about reincarnation and her belief about her soul being reborn over and over again. I was next, and found myself saying, "The God I serve has such power, such creative ability, that He doesn't need to recycle souls. We are each a unique and special individual." The Holy Spirit must have spoken. A young man across from me, who labeled himself a "lapsed Catholic," was almost blown over backwards in his seat. This red-headed young man turned white as a sheep. I think Someone had spoken to his heart. I long to find out, when I get to heaven, what happened to the people from this type of witnessing opportunity. Jesus never wastes an opening, and I was determined to take advantage of each one that came to me.

12.

Back in School Again

I noticed there was something different going on when I arrived one Sabbath at the church, the Japanese church that I had been attending for almost four years now. People were in small groups, talking and shaking their heads. Some supporting each other. What happened? A great man in the Japanese Adventist community had died. His name was Kinichi Nozaki. He had just passed his one hundredth birthday. He was the first Japanese Adventist pastor in the United States. In the early 1900s, he came to America to learn modern farming techniques. On the way across the Pacific to Victoria, BC, Canada, he had an experience akin to some of the seafaring adventures of the apostle Paul. He was 750 miles from Canada when the propeller on his steamer broke. With no equipment to send a distress signal, the ship floated for several days before encountering a major storm that almost sank the ship. Miraculously, a large ship found them and towed them to shore. From Canada he continued his trip to San Francisco, California.

From there, he embarked and began a new life in America, where he decided to remain. He had problems establishing himself, however. He had difficulty finding work because of prejudice. He met a Seventh-day Adventist lady named Mrs. Swift, who gave English lessons in the community. In the wake of the prejudice he was encountering, her kindness drew him. She also taught a Bible study once a week. He used this opportunity to further his knowledge of English. The Spirit did its work and he met Jesus.

Kinichi and another man decided to go to the college at Loma Linda to become Bible workers. After the one-year course, he started evangelizing Japanese farmers by bicycling all over Central California. He was a tireless worker and ended up establishing many of the Japanese Adventist churches between British Columbia and Peru. During World War II, he and his family were interned in one of the camps that the US government had set up after the attack on Pearl Harbor. Stories abound about how he used that horrible situation to find many lost sheep among the detainees, holding as many as eight Bible studies a day. The reaction to his death was deep because many of the members had met Jesus through his ministry. He pastored the churches in Mountain View and San Francisco for many years, churches that he had founded.

A large memorial service was planned, with an intensive effort to invite those who were touched by Pastor Nozaki's ministry. When the service took place, the church was overflowing. Scores had traveled many miles to attend a service filled with tears and joy. At the end, Pastor Nozaki's extended family met a long line of visitors to receive condolences. As the family lined up, I was surprised to see Carolyn, the lady I had met in Yosemite. She was just as cute as I remembered. It turned out she was Pastor Nozaki's granddaughter. She was very busy at the banquet that followed; everybody seemed to know her. As the banquet wound down, we were able to renew our acquaintance for several minutes. She says I mentioned that she should "visit more often" (I don't remember saying that). It turns out, too, that I had met her parents and brother and sister months before ever meeting her.

A few months later, Carolyn visited the church again, this time with her parents. For some reason, there wasn't a potluck planned that week. Carolyn's aunt and uncle, my closest friends, invited me to their home. I had been there before and looked forward to savory vegetarian cuisine, Asian style. It was the first time that Carolyn and I spent some extended time together. We talked after lunch and went for a walk in the neighborhood. No fireworks went off, but I was curious about what looked like, maybe, God's hand at work. God's leading me to the Japanese church, my becoming familiar with Asian culture, the casual meeting at Yosemite, finding out that she was related to my best friends, meeting again at the memorial service, and her visit to the church, leading to lunch together. *Coincidence?*

Before I left that afternoon, we traded addresses and decided to write to each other. (No email back then.) After a few rounds of letters, I pushed for using the phone. I didn't like writing; I had enough writing to do, completing papers for school (also no word processing). When there was a break in classes, I visited her in Southern California, where she was working as a school physician. We enjoyed phone conversations and occasional visits. Having attended medical school, she understood my struggles with grad school and my lack of time for social activity. Then, with spring break approaching in my fourth semester; I decided to surprise her by coming down for an unannounced visit. I conspired with her mother to make sure she would be at her apartment when I arrived. My plan worked out perfectly, and there I was, standing in her doorway—much to her amazement. My surprise visit seemed to urge our budding relationship forward. *Your will be done, Lord. Your will be done.*

As our relationship progressed, my experience with a failed marriage loomed larger and larger. After my divorce, I had a healthy regard for the marital bond. As I mentioned earlier, soon after my divorce, I was wounded, a bit deceived, and I wanted to get married right away. But God mercifully intervened through circumstances and giving me sound information on healing from a divorce. When someone in one of my classes gave a presentation on the dynamics of a strong marriage, I had doubts. I wasn't comfortable thinking about the commitment of marriage. With summer break coming, Carolyn and I planned to start visiting each other more often, every two weeks, in fact. I would go down for a visit, then she would come up two weeks later. We were getting together twice a month. We continued this schedule even after my fifth semester started.

My third and fourth semesters went well. I was both astonished and humbled by what Jesus had been enabling me to do. I was healing, too. My confidence was rising as I continued to complete my assignments. As my confidence grew, my anxiety and fear decreased a little. One of the goals of cognitive-behavioral therapy (CBT) is to change unhelpful thoughts (distortions) and improve emotional control (feelings). Cognitive distortions (the big lie, in my case) were being broken down as I achieved some success. This led to a decrease in my emotional upheavals. Not completely, but enough to realize that I was changing. Jesus was using Spirit-led CBT to bring progress in my educational outlook and healing to my soul. Amen! Praise the "Wonderful, Counselor ... Prince of Peace" (Isa. 9:6). I was truly experiencing more peace.

Because of the choice I had made in the second semester, to spread out my class load over another year, I had a lighter load than I did the previous two semesters. The fifth semester consisted of two classes. One was a research class for my thesis. This allowed me a little more time to spend with Carolyn. We continued our travel strategy and constant phone time. As I went through the program, the thought of the final barrier—my thesis—would trouble me from time to time. My concept of a thesis was exaggerated, as I remembered a friend who'd had a traumatic experience with hers. I was relieved by my choice to spread classes out.

Though I was pleased with that decision, I was having some second thoughts about the other decision I had made at about the same time. Changing from marriage and family to another program seemed like the right thing to do at the time. My impatience caused me to make a choice that would have a ramification down the road. At the time, all I could see was a very long road to obtaining a license. I also noticed that every oral presentation touching on marriage or family grabbed my interest the most. This interest would always bring to mind the decision I made. But it was too late to change back. So I began including that decision in my prayers. During those last two semesters nothing happened that I would call an answer to my prayers. God answers every prayer, but He reserves the right of *when* to answer. His timing is faultless.

On the home front, the Holy Spirit started working on my mother. For almost four years, she had watched me taking part in spiritual disciplines, studying my Bible, and preparing lessons and sermons. One Sabbath, as I was preaching, Carolyn's aunt, without my knowledge, brought my mother to hear me preach. I imagine that was a high point in her life, to see her son standing in a pulpit. Even if they rarely attended church, people in her generation almost automatically thought themselves to be Christians. What a thoughtful thing for Carolyn's aunt to do.

One day I came across an old Dukane projector in a closet at the church. Before any type of video was available, the projector was a popular tool in Bible Studies. A set of film strips came with the projector, consisting of a set of Bible studies. I decided to take it and see if I could interest my mother in the film strips. Prayerfully, I took the projector home and asked her if she was interested. She was, much to my delight. With her arthritic hands it was nearly impossible for her to load the projector. So I would get the film strip loaded and running for her. I was surprised that she was diligent in watching the strips.

When she finished the strips, I asked her if she wanted to start reading the Bible. To my amazement, she was interested. I got her an easy-to-read Bible and placed some markers in various places in the Scripture. I spent some time explaining the difference between the Old and New Testaments, the Psalms and the Gospels. Watching her struggle with her hands broke my heart. But she kept at it and learned how to use the eraser end of a pencil to turn pages. I would come home sometimes to find her reading on her own. God is unbelievably merciful, and I hope the Spirit was able to plant a seed in her heart. God can take only one seed and nurture it into eternal life.

Upon starting the research class, I had to do some quick searches to get a better handle on what a thesis was. I found that there were different categories, depending on the requirements of the university or college. I was challenged by the variety. Me, writing a thesis? How could this be? Though I had come a long way in my school journey, I still struggled when I encountered something new. And a thesis was a new hurdle, a high one at that. I felt a profound need, which led to some serious prayer time. "Hear my prayer, O LORD, give ear to my supplications! In your faithfulness answer me, *and* in Your righteousness" (Ps. 143:1).

> *Jesus had bailed me out many times because of my poor choices. Before I met Jesus, my life was going nowhere because of poor, selfish choices.*

My anxiety was higher than it had been in a while. I didn't know how to pick a topic or how much or what kind of research I would have to do. The research professor was helpful in that area and the class received a substantial packet of instructions. But I had no idea what I was going to focus on for a topic. I was supposed to decide on a topic as soon as possible after the class started. What should I do? In rereading some material about the types of thesis, I focused on what was called a *project*. This appealed to me because no statistics would be involved. I wouldn't have to prove or disprove a theory or premise. Avoiding statistics sounded good.

So I decided on doing a project. It would require a long essay or dissertation on the topic I chose. My anxiety level softened when I made that choice. No statistics! Next, I needed to pick a topic. I was urged in the class to pick something I would be extremely interested in because of the amount of time that would be spent on the topic. The professor made it clear to the class that the department would be flexible with our choices. I went to the library and looked at a selection of old projects to get some ideas. They were helpful in giving me some general ideas but no real help on a specific topic. I continued praying. Another student was having a hard time also, and so we had some brainstorming conversations. He was struggling more than I was. The second time we talked, he grumbled that he had always had poor decision-making skills. That resonated with me. I knew that in that area, my skills could certainly be better. Jesus had bailed me out many times because of my poor choices. Before I met Jesus, my life was going nowhere because of poor, selfish choices. The big lie in my life, my false beliefs, hampered my ability to make good decisions.

I decided to do something with *decision making*. What was I going to do with that topic? I had no idea! I talked to the professor about the possibilities. He was very encouraging and gave me the name of a periodical that might help. The encouragement was beneficial, but I still needed to narrow down what I was going to do with the topic. I thanked God for the progress I was making and continued to pray specifically. The next week the professor announced that each student would be assigned an advisor who would shepherd us through the final process. Of course, I immediately started praying, for this would be a very important step in completing my thesis.

When we were assigned to an advisor, I was disappointed. The advisor was the statistics professor I'd had earlier. He was old, soon to be retiring. Sometimes in class he was a little forgetful and at times, didn't seem too interested. He was one of the reasons I found statistics was extra difficult. I didn't know if I could request another advisor or not.

This was a big dilemma at a very important juncture in my program. Of course, I didn't know if he would be helpful or not. I decided I would rely on Jesus' answering my prayers. Here I was nearing the end of my journey, and He hadn't let me down once. Not once! So I made an appointment with the professor. My topic remained undecided and vague. When I arrived at his office, we talked for a while. I liked him, felt comfortable. He was easy to talk to. I told him I had decided on doing a project for my thesis. Then I voiced what I was thinking of doing. He was as encouraging as the other professor had been. I informed him that I was having trouble narrowing down the topic. I mentioned the periodical the other professor had recommended. The issue of the periodical I looked at in the library had some decision-making models. When I said that, he responded, "Why don't you make your own model?"

That caught me by surprise. It seemed there must be a number of models already out there. I said, "I'm supposed to write something kind of original, aren't I?"

We decided that I should spend some more time doing research and we would meet in a few days. That sounded good. It would give me more time to investigate. And to pray. I spent time in the library without getting any specific direction. There seemed to be ample information on decision-making and several models already devised. My advisor suggested that I try to find a niche, something that appealed to me and had some personal meaning.

Like the other professor, he had said it was important to find something I would enjoy, because I would live with it for months. Later, I thought about what was important to me, what had personal meaning. What came to mind didn't surprise me. It was what I was interested in most—the Bible!

The notion of doing a thesis on a Christian topic at a secular university, in a program heavily influenced by New Age philosophy, was daunting.

Well, wouldn't that be something? What coalesced in my mind was stimulating: *A Decision-making model based on the Bible*. I could get into something like that! I hadn't seen anything even close to that perspective in my preliminary searches. It would be a niche, and something with personal meaning.

But then reality set in. Would my advisor allow me to do something so overtly religious? Would the Bible be accepted as a legitimate source? Things were rushing through my mind. I thanked Jesus for the ideas and began praying for His will to be done. Well, wouldn't that topic be something?

I called my advisor and made an appointment for the following day. I thought and prayed about how I should introduce my idea. I even went so far as to write down some notes to keep me focused. The notion of doing a thesis on a Christian topic at a secular university, in a program heavily influenced by New Age philosophy, was daunting. But two thoughts came to mind. The first was that the research professor had told the class the department would be flexible in accepting topics. The second was Jesus. If His hand was in this choice, then it would work out. If not, then He had something better for me.

As we sat down in his office, I was feeling anxious but hopeful. After some small talk, I told him that I had found something that interested me. That I would have no trouble "living with it" for the next few months. When I told him my topic, he seemed to come alive, as if receiving a shot of adrenalin. For the first time I saw a gleam in his eye. The old professor became animated, so different from the way he had been in class.

"You must be a Christian?" he asked, very affably.

When I said that I was, he relaxed back in his chair and seemed quite pleased.

"I am, too," he said, with a sense of satisfaction.

He was very excited about my topic and couldn't wait to be involved.

"This will," he said, "top off my last semester here," a reference to his impending retirement. He looked forward to being able to talk about spiritual things because, he said, "I'm the only Christian on the staff."

The only one—and I was assigned to him!

Thank you, Jesus. How could I not see, again, the reality of the Lord working in my life. As usual, however, I had some anxiety. My faith wasn't at the point where some ambiguity was okay. I still needed to feel less in control of situations. I was still learning that Jesus had full control of my life and circumstances. That there was nothing He didn't have control of, no situation, no happenstance, no arrow from the adversary. You would think that after the events of the last couple of years, I would have a rock-solid faith. But I didn't.

I remembered the struggles of the Israelites as they wandered in the desert for forty years. Their faith wavered as they encountered new and vague circumstances, time and again. By God's mercy and grace, they finally made it to the Promised Land. And I needed to find out that His mercy and grace would see me through, also. Would it take forty years? Would I have to go through failures like Israel? Does victory ultimately come through failure? I think the answer is yes, victory comes through failure *if* we confess and learn to be honest with Jesus about our sin and allow Him to take care of every situation. To this day, I am growing in this area.

Now I needed to hit my thesis—head on. Libraries became a second home. The library at San Jose State had a surprising number of books dealing with decision making. Also, religious-based books and some periodicals. I gleaned what I could from them. I went to the local library in my hometown, which had little to offer from an academic perspective.

Meeting with my advisor was always beneficial in two ways. One, I reaped valuable direction for the different aspects of my thesis from his long career in education. Two, we developed a kinship through our common beliefs and fellowship. He was a staunch Lutheran. He shared with me his current struggle with the impending split of his beloved church over the role of women. It was weighing heavily on him.

It was his encouragement and direction that put me over the top in my research. He urged me to visit the Graduate Theological Union Library at University of California, Berkley. I hit paydirt! A whole library dedicated to the field of religion. There was a vast area dedicated to Christianity. I was thankful I had learned firsthand that Jesus knew every page of every book in that library. The first visit was a real education on some of the basics of research. I sat in awe of the students who were there. They seemed to know exactly what they were doing. Whizzing through the stacks, finding what they were looking for. Zooming through the microfiche at blinding speed. And they had mastered the art of photocopying large numbers of pages rapidly. I picked up some good pointers from just sitting there and watching them. Immediately, I saw I wasn't prepared because I hadn't brought any quarters for the copier. Fortunately, the lady pointed me to a dollar changer situated in a corner behind her desk. I had an answer to prayer by finding lots of excellent material. Over the next three months, I returned three more times.

The more I followed the thesis guidelines, the more complex the project became. The thesis required three chapters before getting to the model itself. These chapters were "Introduction," "Review of Related Literature," and "Design and Methodology." These chapters alone were much more than I had ever researched and written before. I was doing all this work in the research class in my fifth semester. The research professor counseled us to look at the work one chapter at a time. Regrettably, the research information didn't come in the same sequence as the chapters. I had to set up file folders to keep everything organized. *How did I ever do that?* It helped my anxiety to be getting ahead of the game. Or at least it felt that way.

With my advisor's guidance, I was making progress. After the first three chapters came "Results and Findings," followed by the chapters "Discussion" and "Conclusion." The last requirement was an abstract. It is the last item written, but it is the first part of the thesis. It is a brief summary of the thesis and it is used to help the reader quickly ascertain the purpose of the thesis. I read many of them. That fifth semester ended, and all I had left in my last semester was to finish writing my thesis. God had richly blessed with my adviser and my research. I had two main thoughts on my mind. The thesis, of course, and Carolyn.

During that fifth semester, we continued our occasional visits and ample phone time. I kept her up to speed with what was happening with my thesis. I did find time to go down south on an extended weekend. Without telling me, she had made arrangements for us to attend a conference focusing on righteousness by faith. It was interesting and a great opportunity to spend time doing something together. We agreed that our relationship was ripening. It was a reluctant flight home after the weekend. But I had to keep hammering away, page after page.

When my last semester started, I barely had to go to the university, except to see my advisor and the library. The bulk of my research was nearly complete. The thesis was going well, and my advisor was having a great time reading each chapter and giving input. Mainly, what I had to do was keep my nose to the grindstone. When I hit fifty written pages, I was amazed because I was just beginning chapter four, the *results and findings* chapter, where I would actually begin constructing my model. I spent some extra time in prayer as I began. I really felt I didn't know what I was doing. I kept praying, and my adviser kept encouraging me. I kept writing.

The semester went by quickly, and my thesis was done before the deadline. It turned out to be eighty-six pages typed. My advisor loved it. It was accepted and I was finished with my program. Praise God! I had, by His grace, done it!

A few weeks remained in the semester, so I decided to take a job with a private driving school to earn some money. My scholarship was up, and I needed to save for whatever was my next step. What that next step was, I had no idea. I was praying, but Jesus had given no indication. So I earned a state license as a behind-the-wheel driving instructor. I quickly built up my meager checking account and learned a great deal about people's fear. I, then, had graduated from San Jose State University. My grade point average was 3.8, the statistics class being my only B.

What now, about the next steps? What *was* the next step? What was going to happen with my mother? That four-month stay had turned into four years—and counting. What about new career opportunities? Driving instruction was only a short-term money maker. And what about Carolyn? Yes, Jesus, what about Carolyn? Now that I was out of school, we were able to spend more time together. The airlines loved us. She surprised me by showing up unannounced at the Lay Evangelist Training Seminar (LETS) at Soquel. Everything was going well. I had doubled my prayer time about our relationship. But there was no clear direction or answer. I was encouraged by Psalm 37:7, "Rest in the LORD, and wait patiently for Him." For once, that was fairly easy to do because I could see how arrangements would have to be made concerning my mother. Yes, there were some issues that needed to be resolved for me to be able to move on.

The summer came not long after graduation. That meant most of the schools Carolyn worked at were out for the summer. Only a couple were year round. This gave her some time off, which we made good use of. The best outing was at Soquel Camp Meeting. She stayed in a tent with a friend of mine from the Sunnyvale church. It gave me an opportunity to tell her about some of the miracles that had happened there, which led me to San Jose State. It was a great ten-day run with many spiritual blessings;

Carolyn enjoyed seeing some old friends from her college days. That was one of the best aspects of camp meeting. Also, it was the longest uninterrupted time we had spent together. We both were comfortable with where we were in our relationship. She understood the complications of my mother's situation. I continued to pray and work. I also started wrestling with thoughts about my future, along with the decision I had made early in my program at San Jose State. I was thinking more and more that I had made a mistake in not pursuing the Marriage and Family degree. I asked Jesus for clarification.

It didn't take long for Him to answer my prayers. One night, I received a call from a friend asking me if I would talk with a newly married couple having problems. I agreed. Upon meeting, I realized that I was in over my head; there were significant issues here. But they were so needy, and so wanting help, that I couldn't tell them to find someone else. I ended up meeting with them several times. I'm not sure how much I helped in their case, but I realized that working with marital problems was where I wanted to be.

Though a neophyte, I was both comfortable and stimulated by being in the moment with this couple, and I became convicted that I had been mistaken in changing the emphasis of my program. There I was again, letting one of my weaknesses get the better of my situation. My impatience overruled my faith that God would see me through, that He had a plan for me—no matter how far away it seemed. This was a huge, almost crushing, lesson for me to learn.

Now what? Had I wasted three years of sweat and tears?

I confessed to Jesus my lack of faith over the decision and asked what I should do. A thought occurred to me; since I did have a degree, I felt I needed to explore opportunities to help people in transition. I decided to look deeper into the field and see what the employment opportunities were. I spent some time researching what kind of jobs would be available to me. All of the jobs were of a rehab nature, mostly state and federal positions, some hospital. It would be helping people who needed to restart their lives, or were undergoing transition because of change in circumstances. In searching for specific job openings, I was let down to find that there wasn't much available in my area. I wasn't sure whether I should be disappointed or not. Maybe it was for the better that this employment avenue was closed. I wanted to give Jesus as much breadth as possible to lead me out of the mess I had created, so I decided to continue checking for opportunities.

I needed to apprise Carolyn about my dilemma, about this new bump in the road of my life, a life that now involved my deepening relationship with her. Sympathetic, she told me about a similar situation she went through after graduating from medical school. She had felt burnt out on medicine and decided to take some time off, instead of going into the mandatory one-year internship. After a number of months, she realized that it was a mistake to get behind in her progress toward residency. It wasn't easy to slip back into an internship. She did a one-year internship in pediatrics, which didn't seem to be a fit for her. So she took a position with Los Angeles Unified School District as a school physician. That sequence of events helped her better understand my dilemma.

Over the next few months, I continued to pray and to work, to take care of my mother, and to nurture my relationship with Carolyn. We continued to move ever closer. We were together for Christmas and New Year's. I began seriously praying about marriage. Carolyn came up again at the end of January for my birthday. We went to dinner on one of the days she was there. I had made the big decision to ask her to be my wife. I made reservations at a fabulous Chinese restaurant. Before she arrived, I did something creative. (At least, I thought it was creative! Not easy for someone as uncreative as I am.) I decided to ask for her hand through a fortune cookie.

I don't know where the zany scheme came from. I used the secretary's typewriter at work to make two fortunes. The secretary loved being in on something "so romantic." I had bought some fortune cookies and carefully pulled out the fortunes with tweezers. It took me only seven broken cookies before success. Then, I gingerly squeezed my proposal into the two cookies (I wanted to make sure she would get the proposal whichever one she chose). The fortune read, *A tall man with a beard is asking you to marry him.* When we arrived at the restaurant, I made an excuse to talk to the hostess. She was happy to make sure the two cookies would be placed on our table at the proper time. After the meal, the cookies arrived with the bill. I was tingling with anticipation. When she cracked the cookie open and read the fortune, and then read the fortune again, she glowingly said, "Yes"! I'm sure the full house enjoyed our kiss almost as much as we did.

We floated around for a couple of days. We dropped by her aunt and uncle's before I took Carolyn to the airport. Of course, we also informed my mother of the happy occasion. I hadn't told her ahead of time because I thought she might unintentionally give things away. Upon returning from the airport, the wide array of obstacles, logistics, problems, and complications were swirling around my mind. I was a little overwhelmed even though plans hadn't even been discussed yet.

One situation took a twist when my mother was given a new medication. She had gone through several courses of treatment over the previous fifteen years. In those years "modern" medicine didn't know much about the management of rheumatoid arthritis, especially a severe case like hers. This new treatment was a series of shots. Shots of pure gold! She had tried so many treatments that I didn't think much about this new one. But within a couple of months, almost unbelievable healing began taking place. Her stainless-steel knees and plastic knuckles weren't repaired, of course. But her flexibility, dexterity, and energy increased tremendously. She was better than I had seen her in years. This gave me hope that arrangements could be made for her care and I would be free to go wherever God would lead. I wondered if the Great Physician had a hand in the timing and efficacy of her treatment.

I also started praying about what to do with my education blunder. It was obvious I had made a terrible mistake in changing my program. Impatience is a serious sin. It's nothing more than selfishness. *I want it and I want it now!* When impatience and fear rule, they are vile taskmasters. In my case, it caused unnecessary delay and confusion in moving forward with God's plan. I'm so grateful that Jesus always has a plan B. He loves bailing out thickheaded sinners like me. Before getting engaged, I was wondering if I could re-enroll at San Jose State and take the remaining courses in marriage and family. With the engagement, that possibility was out the window. With Carolyn working in Southern California, it looked like I was going to be moving there at some point. So the engagement effectively ended a possible return to San Jose State.

With God, situations sometimes change rapidly. When God's timing has come, nothing can stop Him. This seemed to be the case with our engagement. We had made no plans for when I would move to Southern California, if that was His plan. There were really no plans for what I would be doing there, or when the wedding would be. We were just basking in the glow of our recent decision. The only possibility that occurred to me, if I was going to follow my conviction to be a marriage and family counselor, would be to go back to school! The ramifications of a poor choice had far-reaching consequences on my life, and now Carolyn's. What an added problem for me to work through. There were already several circumstances that needed to be addressed for Carolyn and me to be in the same locale. My future career path was an unneeded addition. But what could I do?

The next month, I flew south to visit my fiancée. That term, *fiancée*, seemed to fit easily into my emotional system. It felt right. I continued to discuss my issue with Carolyn. We agreed that another grad school was a viable option, though not my favorite one. But if returning to school was the only way I could rectify my mistake, then so be it. We were together for the first time as a couple at the condo she had bought several months before. A nice 650-square-foot abode in Glendale for us to begin our life together.

While there, I started looking for information about local graduate schools that offered degrees in marriage and family. This was before Google, so information wasn't readily available. I found a couple of local colleges and had information sent to my home. I also found one in, of all places, the Yellow Pages, and had them send information too. Later, I found two additional schools, which were Christian universities. Even though I was living in the San Francisco Bay Area, I was a bit overwhelmed by the vastness of Southern California. Two of the schools later proved to be too far away. But I received five brochures and grad-school information from the schools, so that I could compare. A few days after returning home, I received a call from Carolyn. It seemed that it was God's time to begin revealing His plan for our future.

13.

Carolyn

Sometimes Jesus uses a routine event, a phone call, a text message, or an email to set His plans in motion. This is what happened to Carolyn and me when she heard at the monthly staff meeting that the school-physician program was going to be hit with mass layoffs in the fall. It was part of the fallout from extended labor negotiations between the school district and the local teachers' union. Carolyn's program was being cut back, leaving only a few of the supervisors. To a room full of doctors, this was a shock. It shook us also. We had made no specific plans in the few weeks we had been engaged. Carolyn's news, however, opened up new options for us. Finding out which path Jesus wanted us to follow was an important element in our newly-joined walk. Bringing two lives together gives Jesus an opportunity to lead in new directions. It had seemed that I was going to move south. But now other scenarios were possible. We both started praying for Jesus' plan to manifest itself.

Even though there were a few months remaining in the current school year, the doctors were encouraged to begin looking for other employment. So Carolyn sent up a quick prayer right there in the meeting, about options. Because she hadn't gone through a residency, she didn't have a specialty. She had struggled with finding her niche, a field that fit. One of the main functions of a physician in her school district was to interview families in an attempt to discover any family or environmental

Wrong choices certainly can have vast repercussions.

issues that might be causing a child to act out in school. Maybe the child was disrupting class, challenging the teacher, fighting, or starting fires in garbage cans; in the extreme, bringing a gun to school. Finding the cause, such as bullying, the parent's impending divorce, or a sibling's terminal illness, can begin alleviating the problem. She found that she really enjoyed the interviewing process, the search to uncover the issues affecting the student. Almost every day Carolyn drove by Los Angeles

County Hospital going to and from work. She knew that the University of Southern California Medical School joined with the hospital for their residency program in psychiatry. After the announcement at the staff meeting, she found herself taking the off-ramp to the hospital on the way home. She decided to stop in at the hospital and pick up some information about their psychiatry program.

As we meander through life, walking with Jesus, we never know when we are entering into a divine appointment of God's making. Carolyn certainly didn't know. She was just stopping in to pick up some information as she was seeking God's direction. It seems God had additional plans. As she was talking to the program secretary, the director walked out of his office and heard their conversation. To make a long story short, the director spent time showing her the facility and informing Carolyn about the requirements of the program. He also told her that the match process had already taken place and he still had two openings. Match Day happens once a year and determines which residency new doctors are accepted into to pursue a specialty. It was rare to have openings after matching was over. The director told her that he could accept her, at this late date, if she could produce the required paperwork and recommendations from Loma Linda Medical School within two weeks. Amazingly, she was able to contact former professors and receive their recommendations in time.

> *I had learned a tremendous lesson about letting my fear and impatience affect a decision.*

Carolyn's residency program would start on July 1, 1989. This obvious providence gave us some direction toward our future. It seemed logical, then, that I would be moving south as we had assumed before Carolyn's job status changed. I flew down for a visit and we made a big decision. It was clear that if I wanted to get back on track and be a marriage and family counselor, the only avenue available would be to go through another program, earn another degree.

Yikes! Wrong choices certainly can have vast repercussions. But what else could I do? *What else could I do?* I had learned a tremendous lesson about letting my fear and impatience affect a decision. I realized that the decision that I had previously made was coming back to haunt me. The extended time to achieve a license, which I'd wanted to avoid, was now going to be a reality, and then some. "The fear of man brings a snare, but whoever trusts in the LORD shall be safe" (Prov. 29:25). Obviously, in this instance I hadn't trusted Jesus. I had let my fear and impatience sway my decision. Oh! How I need Jesus and the healing He offers.

We decided that I would begin gathering more-specific information about the graduate schools I had found, and apply to all of them, as soon as possible. The ones who accepted me would give me a pool to choose from. I was confident that, if it were God's plan, I would end up at the school that was best for me. I resorted to one of my favorite promises in times of uncertainty and lack of clarity. "Call to Me, and I will answer you, and show you great and mighty things, which you do not know" (Jer. 33:3). Remarkable promise! I didn't know which school was best, but Jesus did. Making a decision sometimes leads to more decisions. Of course, we had a plethora of decisions to make in order for me to move south, get married, find work, and start school. Each of these decisions would lead to more decisions. Actually, some information I learned from my thesis helped in the decision-making process. I had peace from the certainty that none of the impending decisions were beyond God's reach.

It occurred to me that starting a new master's program at the end of summer meant that I needed to move south beforehand. This realization brought another weighty thought. Where would I live? That would be quite an expense. I had saved a considerable amount from working, but I'd wanted to use it for tuition. My prudent wife-to-be immediately understood the ramifications of my moving before we were married. After praying about the dilemma, we decided that the best way to handle the situation would be for us to get married before Carolyn started her residency in July. This decision settled most of the moving dilemma, but brought up more. The biggest was the wedding. There were just a few months before Carolyn would start her program, and a month or so later for me.

Ordinarily, wedding plans are started a year or more ahead of the date. We had far less time, and a further complication was finding an outdoor wedding location, which I knew Carolyn coveted. We talked about it, and she agreed to start making calls the next day. She told me that some plans were already being addressed by her mother and sister and some church friends. From my time at the Mountain View church, I knew that organizing an event was a real strength in the Japanese community, and Carolyn knew many people in the local Japanese church community. I flew home that evening with many thoughts running through my head. Significant changes had happened in that short visit. The first issue that needed to be addressed when I was back home was my mother's care. She continued to do well with her new treatment. She was happy about the marriage and made insinuations about my moving on. I didn't see it that clearly. Who would buy her groceries, take her to the doctor, and take care of all the other matters of daily living? As I recalled all that had happened since the engagement, I was comforted by the knowledge that Jesus had a solution to my mother's situation as part of His overall plan for my new life. And He did. My sister offered to be more involved in our mother's care. During the time I was living with my mother, one of my sister's kids had moved out of the house and the second was just about out the door. So she would have more time to watch over our mother. It never ceases to amaze me how Jesus' plans work out if we allow Him to have His way. "I have come that they may have life, and they may have *it* more abundantly" (John 10:10).

About two months passed and Carolyn still hadn't found a location for the wedding. As far as I knew, the rest of the preparation was going well. My part was fairly easy compared to what had to happen down south. I had the groomsmen lined up, and I reserved the tuxedos and did whatever else Carolyn asked me to do. Carolyn called all over Southern California to every location she knew of and to others that had been suggested to her. All were booked many months in advance. One day at work she was talking to her nurse about the predicament. The nurse suggested she call the Glendale Recreation Department and inquire about Brand Park. The nurse had attended an event there months before. Carolyn called and asked whether they had any outdoor locations where a wedding of more than 100 people could be held. Carolyn was elated when they said they had a beautiful spot on their grounds. She couldn't believe her ears when she was told they had a Japanese tea garden. Glendale had joined with a city in Japan as "sister cities," and that involved trading cultural icons from their respective countries. The tea garden was part of that exchange. It was beautiful, with a Koi pond, a beautiful Japanese garden, and a large tea house with many shade trees. It would be a perfect place to hold the wedding.

The big question remained: Did they have an opening? Carolyn was told that they had one opening! Of course, we needed it before July 1, when she would begin her residency. The chances of that were slim. Carolyn was ecstatic when they told her the opening was on June 18. She made sure to clarify they were talking about this year. They said yes and added that she had a choice of times. Ten o'clock in the morning or three o'clock in the afternoon. She reserved the ten o'clock opening. As it turned out, Brand Park was only about a mile and a half from Carolyn's condo. *Was that reservation left open by happenstance, or had the God of heaven kept it open for two of His children?* How could I not believe the latter?

While all the planning and preparation for the wedding was going on, I was applying to graduate schools. All five of the schools I contacted sent me information and an application. I decided to apply to all five, even the two which were farther than I would want to drive. I wanted to give Jesus as much room as He needed. I just couldn't make another mistake; I had messed up enough. The program I had found in the yellow pages was different from the others. It was a private, free-standing program, not affiliated with a university. I was hopeful to find the right one and enroll so I would have one less issue to contend with as I anticipated my move. My issues with fear and anxiety seemed to be greatly diminished, but I wasn't facing a classroom yet.

My healthy regard for marriage hadn't abated upon getting engaged. The adversary brought in all kinds of reasons to doubt. I couldn't become a two-time loser. Even though Jesus had given ample evidence that He was involved, I still struggled. Wounds from divorce run deep. I talked about it with Carolyn. We really wanted to know, as best we could, that God was going to bless our marriage. At the very least, that it was okay with Him. We both had some understanding of the sacredness of marriage, a holy institution. We talked quite a bit about it and prayed profusely. I felt I needed all the help I could get in making the second most important decision there is, picking the life partner. The only more important choice is, of course, accepting Jesus into your heart. We thought that God had answered our prayers in two ways. First, with the last-minute reservation at Brand Park and, second, the acceptance into my choice of graduate program.

Yes, I was looking for more confirmation. Maybe I was being overly conscientious, but marriage is a big deal. Being a failure in my first try, I wanted to be comfortable with my decision. Carolyn understood and was in agreement. So we started holding up two "fleeces" before the throne of grace. When we secured the Tea Garden, we were so thankful. That only left grad school. He really tested my faith on this one. He did not make it easy. After I applied, I began scrutinizing the material they had sent and comparing programs. The more I studied the programs, the more I was drawn to the private program called California Family Study Center (CALFAM). It had components in its program that the others didn't. It was *very* different from San Jose State. It was more clinically oriented. CALFAM was a two-fold enterprise. The second story of the building was the school, including a library. The first floor was a counseling center where all the teachers had their practice. This was very appealing to me. Classes would be taught by working counselors, not academic teachers. Also, their scheduling was attractive. One full day a week of classes and a half day of practical clinical issues, where we would, among other things, watch actual therapy happening through a one-way mirror. None of the other schools offered anything even close. I decided to focus on that program, while still being open to God's leading elsewhere. Also, CALFAM's scheduling would make it easier to find part-time work.

About a month or so before the wedding, I was still waiting for an answer about grad school. I had called the two schools that were a great distance from Glendale and asked them to drop me from consideration. That left CALFAM and two others. Every day I went to the mailbox hoping to hear something from someone. I asked God why He was taking so long. I felt I needed an answer. "But be not discouraged if your prayers do not seem to obtain an immediate answer... Men pray for that which will gratify their selfish desires, and the Lord does not fulfill their requests in the way which they expect. He takes them through tests and trials" (White, *In Heavenly Places*, p. 89).

Well, trials it was. This was the last block we needed to fall into place. But what if I didn't hear anything? Maybe this was a lack of faith, I don't know. I decided to call the registrars at the various schools. Of course, I had to leave messages at all three. It was helpful to remember what I learned at San Jose State; how God is involved even with the inner-workings of school administrations. Long story short, one of the universities never called back. Another asked me if I had received a letter from them saying I was put on a waiting list for the following semester. I hadn't. I would have relished that, for it would have narrowed the field. CALFAM was the only one left. But they didn't return my call, either. I called again and left another message.

A thought hit me. Maybe I wasn't going to go to school after all. Maybe God had another plan and I had missed His leading again. Not a good feeling. But this time CALFAM called back. I identified myself and explained to the woman why I was calling and my need for an answer. After putting me on hold for a while, she came back and said, "I'm sorry, I can't find your paperwork, can I call you back?" What could I say? That familiar anxiety started to rise. "My brethren, count it all joy when you fall into various trials, knowing that the testing of your faith produces patience" (James 1:2–3). I have always thought this is one of the more difficult challenges in the Christian life. How do you count it all joy when you trip over a curb carrying takeout, in front of a crowd, tearing your new pants and skinning a knee? At least I didn't cuss.

Two days of waiting for a callback resulted in a marathon prayer offensive. It was reassuring to be in God's presence, unburdening my soul, giving my anxiety to the Great Comforter, who said to us, "Come to Me, all *you* who labor and are heavy laden, and I will give you rest" (Matt. 11:28). Once again, leaning on the promise of God enabled me to make it through this trial. Finally, a call came from CALFAM. The lady apologized profusely for the delay. My paperwork had been found inside someone else's file. The verdict? I had been accepted for the upcoming semester!

We didn't feel that we were testing God but simply looking for a final, heavenly confirmation that Jesus had brought us together and that He would bless our marriage and anoint whatever ministry we would have.

The two "fleeces" had been fulfilled. We didn't feel that we were testing God but simply looking for a final, heavenly confirmation that Jesus had brought us together and that He would bless our marriage and anoint whatever ministry we would have. I have never felt the need to put a fleece before the Lord since that time. He is faithful!

The wedding went off without a hitch. The tea garden was beautiful, as was my new wife! I could tell that all her hopes and expectations were met. The attendees, most of whom were Japanese, were captivated by the surroundings. Jesus truly blessed Carolyn's dreams. The vegetarian Asian food was savory and so abundant that we took a large cooler on our brief honeymoon cruising up the California coast.

Then Carolyn started her residency. I had another month or so until my program started. I began looking for part-time work. It was not easy. The vastness of Southern California combined with my lack of knowledge of the area made the search frustrating. At that time the help-wanted section of the daily paper was the main outlet for looking for work. This was before Google, so it was nearly impossible for me to know how far from Glendale a particular listing was. As usual, I was looking for God's leading. I knew He had a job that would fit my upcoming schedule. After about a month, I was spent. I had found several opportunities, only to learn that they were too far away. Driving anywhere can be a marathon on the Los Angeles freeways. Finally, I answered an ad for part-time work, which advertised flexible hours. That's what I needed. I secured an interview but was disappointed as I drove further and further to the location. The position was in a business that acquired real-estate data for appraisers to do their property evaluations. They had offices all over Southern California. I asked the interviewer where the job opening was. To my surprise and great joy, it was in the Glendale office! How absolutely amazing is my God? The great Creator and Sustainer of the universe is interested enough in my little life to provide employment within one mile of my new home. *One mile!*

The following week I showed up at CALFAM to pay tuition, buy books, and choose my schedule. I have to say the fear and anxiety was there, but not nearly at the level it was when I began at San Jose State. A situation that happened while waiting in line to buy books was very revealing in assessing my emotional state. A very young lady and I struck up a conversation while we waited. Immediately, I could tell she was overwhelmed. As we talked, I heard some of myself in her emotional chatter. She was having a difficult time. I was able to share briefly some of my previous experience at San Jose State. Our little talk seemed to help her a bit, but it helped me even more, in that I realized how much I had grown. I have to admit I felt ready to face whatever came my way. I became a sort of touchstone for this lady as we had the same schedule. Apparently, she handles anxiety way better than I do. She graduated as valedictorian of our class.

So here I was back in school. CALFAM was completely different from San Jose State. Where San Jose State's program was loose and leaned toward education, CALFAM was much more structured and focused on clinical issues. The focus at the beginning of the program was on psychological theory and personality concepts. This was quite challenging for me, as I had no background in any of the models they were introducing. Also, I was determined to be a Christian counselor and little of the information seemed to make sense in the Christian context. As more was introduced, the more frustrated I became. I found myself one night calling out to God and asking Him to just give me a full-time job as a truck driver. He must have heard my prayer and knew I needed some encouragement.

I clearly remember that soon after my praying, a professor introduced the class to family systems theory, a human-behavior theory that focuses on the emotional innerworkings of a family unit; that is, the way in which a family responds to emotions, and the impact of this response on the behavior in the family. I knew by the end of that class this was what I was looking for, because I understood each concept as it was introduced. It just made sense. Praise God! The Bible is full of "family systems" and their effect on individuals, couples, and extended families. Even on Jesus. From then on, I had a basic theory to research for assigned papers. I also learned a great deal about my own family by applying the theory to my "family of origin." For me, this was one of the biggest benefits of going to CALFAM; each paper was part theoretical and part application of the theory to my own family.

The first year passed quicky, and with only a modicum of fear and anxiety. I was surprised by this because the program was much more academically rigorous and went into more depth with family studies than did the program at San Jose State. I studied extra hard to keep up. The second year focused on such topics as individual, couples, and family therapy. Watching actual therapy sessions through the one-way mirror was exciting and instructional. The program ran for two years. This time there was no opportunity to stretch my program out. So in the third semester I began thinking about what I was going to do for my thesis. What I learned about thesis writing at San Jose State turned out to be very helpful. I don't remember why, but I ended up writing on the topic of the initial assessment with a client. The assessment is the foundation on which you begin building the history and forming the diagnosis and course of treatment. The assessment begins with the first contact with a potential client, which is usually on the phone.

As I was heading into the last semester, I realized that there hadn't been any outstanding miracles happen like my experience at San Jose State. Of course, my continued success was an ongoing miracle. But nothing like what had happened at San Jose State. I still was consistently claiming promises and leaning on Jesus for wisdom. One requirement of the fourth quarter was to begin an internship by the semester's end. This meant finding a counseling center that was looking for interns, going through an interview process, and seeing clients as a trainee under supervision. After graduation, a trainee can acquire an intern license, which is the next step to becoming fully licensed. Heavy stuff to be included in an already busy fourth semester. The school provided an intern coordinator to facilitate students' acquiring an internship.

About halfway through the semester, I had an appointment with the coordinator for some needed direction. I told him I was looking for a Christian internship. He said He had never had a request like that. I looked through a large binder he provided and found nothing. I left with a degree of anxiety in my heart and a prayer on my lips.

As we came close to the end of the semester, I had completed my thesis and was focusing on the upcoming finals. I hadn't made any progress in finding an internship and wondered what I was going to do. One day, I heard someone yelling my name from the other end of the corridor. It was the intern coordinator. He was jogging down the hall waving a paper in the air. "I have an internship for you to check out." He told me he'd just received a call out of the blue from a Christian counseling group looking for an intern. They were called the California Christian Counseling Center (Quad C), in Pasadena, which was close to my home. The coordinator was excited for me and gave me the paper, which had all of the information I needed.

I called the Center and arranged an interview. It turned out to be an extensive one. The following day they called and offered me an internship. I started showing up a couple of times a week for training, until school was over. After graduation, I spent a year as a counselor there. I received excellent training by doing cotherapy with a licensed counselor and lots of supervision. Someone told me I was the first Seventh-day Adventist they had hired. I met many solid born-again Christians who were on staff at Quad C. They were from various churches. I thoroughly enjoyed the interplay that went on during staff meetings and between sessions.

So I now had two master's degrees, one in educational counseling and one in marriage and family therapy. An educationally-challenged sinner, deceived by the big lie, struggling with fear and anxiety. Two degrees in a little over five and a half years. *What God has wrought in my life!* I take no glory in what Jesus did in those years. I just stumbled along. The story speaks for itself. I serve a mighty God. A God who is sovereign, the supreme ruler of the universe, and *every* event of my life. A God so powerful that He holds up the whole universe—yet loves me so much that He orchestrated the events of my story.

After a while, something occurred that caused me to pause and contemplate deeply. I toyed with the idea of a different scenario concerning the educational adventure I had just completed. I had looked at my poor choice at San Jose State as a disaster that pulled me off track. I beat myself up pretty intensely. A choice fueled by fear and impatience. A decision that ended up costing me time and an unneeded expenditure of

God's funds for extra tuition. But for some reason, I tried looking at it in a different light. I didn't know if it was correct. I'll have to wait until heaven to find out for sure. It seemed that I was more knowledgeable, more prepared, and more mature spiritually after going through the second program. I don't understand the inner workings of God, but I wondered if in His unfathomable wisdom He knew that I needed both programs.

As I reassessed my time at San Jose State, it seemed to be more of a personal-growth program for me rather than a preparation for a new career. I was so broken, maybe, He knew I needed the healing and growth that the first program would offer. Then I would be better prepared for the more rigorous program at CALFAM. At that point, it was pure conjecture whether this new notion had any validity. Yes, I made the disastrous choice, but it didn't catch Jesus off guard. The bottom line was that I was more prepared as I entered my first internship.

After that year at Quad C, I entered a series of internships, attempting to accumulate the 3,000 hours I needed in order to qualify for the final tests for my license. Yes, those 3,000 hours that had been the crux of my fateful decision at San Jose State. Choices have consequences. But the hours weren't as much a concern as in the past. I had other important factors in my life. A new marriage and another opportunity to glorify God through that union. It was about three months into the marriage that it dawned on us that Jesus had moved us into compatible careers—we were both in the mental-health field. A ministry we could enjoy together. At that time, both of us were busy, with Carolyn's residency and my internships. I would visit her at the hospital when she was on twenty-four-hour call and had to sleep (if you can call it that) there, one of the strains a resident must cope with, to acquire a specialty.

Glendale was a nice, quality city, and we liked the location of our condo. But as with many cities in Southern California back then, crime was rising. During Carolyn's second year of residency, two situations came up, one major and one alarming, both of which started us thinking about moving. The major occurrence was Carolyn's pregnancy. The alarming one was the appearance of graffiti in our neighborhood. Gang activity had begun moving into our area. So we started praying. Our condo association increased security. We couldn't go anywhere immediately, with Carolyn in residency and a baby on the way. It was a busy, exciting time. After our son Jonathan was born on February 6, 1991, Carolyn took six weeks' maternity leave. My hours were in the evening and Carolyn worked during the day, mostly. Carolyn was about halfway through her three-year program. She was enjoying it immensely. After struggling for years, she finally found where God wanted her to be. What a blessing!

Another year passed and we almost moved. We found an immaculate little home in another area in Glendale. We fell in love with it. Prayerfully, we made an offer. But situation after situation, problem after problem occurred, holding up the sale. We didn't understand what was happening. Finally, reluctantly, we had to let that charming house go. At times it is breathtaking to serve a God who knows the future. Six months later, the economy fell apart in Southern California. Government decisions wreaked havoc with the vast defense industry. People were leaving like rats on a sinking ship. Someone told me it was impossible to find a moving van. Property values fell dramatically. If we had purchased that house, we would have been stuck with a very difficult mortgage situation. Jesus had our back! Even our little condo took a significant hit in value. It seemed we weren't going anywhere any time soon.

Carolyn finished her residency and was a newly-minted psychiatrist. She began working part-time for the Los Angeles County Mental Health Department. She worked in East LA, on skid row. She came home with some interesting stories, I must say. Her work with homeless persons and Medicaid clients set a trend that led to our calling, working with the underserved. I continued to accumulate hours toward my license. It was slow going. At one time I was interning with three different counseling centers just to make some progress.

Time passed, and our next-door neighbor revealed that he was selling his condo. It sold in two days for an amount that was more than his asking price. That got us praying about our need to move. When Jonathan arrived, it was easy to accommodate him in our little abode. A crib and chest of drawers in the corner of our bedroom was all we needed. But Carolyn's announcement that she was pregnant again was time for celebration—and conversations about our housing needs. "And my God shall supply all your need . . ." is one of the most important promises for *practical* Christianity, for life's everyday needs (Phil. 4:19). This became our anthem as we began some focused prayer time. After a couple of months, we decided to put our condo up for sale. A realtor began advertising the condo and we started formulating plans to move. We had no indication of what was going to happen. Carolyn had about six months left in her pregnancy, so that gave us some time for Jesus to reveal his plan for us. We were somewhat tied to the LA area because of Carolyn's job situation and the health insurance tied to it.

I have found that it is good to listen to my wife. Sometimes God uses her in particular ways. When, surprisingly, our condo attracted no interest, we were perplexed. Our neighbor had sold so quickly. We found out later that a rich friend had purchased the condo to help him out of a situation. His selling price was not reflective of current property values. We couldn't afford to sell at the going values, so we took it off the market. We slowly developed a plan. We decided to take a trip to Northern California to give God opportunity to reveal His plan for us. With another baby on the way, we needed to move; leaving Southern California was appealing. We prayerfully focused on locations that were near population centers. Because of the nature of our work, we needed people. I mapped out three locations that were appealing and near population centers. We had only four days for the trip, so organization was at a premium. We had beautifully-made resumes and we were going to spread them like the leaves of autumn in these three locations. One night, Carolyn said we needed to include Chico in our trip.

I was not in favor of this suggestion for two reasons. First, after living in Chico, Butte County's major city, for fourteen years, I knew the county had one of the poorest economies in California. Second, additional time and milage would be required to go there. Chico would be the most northerly location to visit, an additional 200 miles round trip. For those reasons, I didn't want to consider Chico. A couple of days later, Carolyn stated that it would be a wasted trip if we didn't investigate Chico.

Her statement had some energy to it. I felt it, and so decided to change plans and include Chico. I think the Spirit spoke to me. This meant changing the whole itinerary I had planned. Chico would have to be the first location, then we would work our way back south to home. The following month we took the trip. The three of us (actually four) piled into our Honda station wagon and headed north. By now I was a little excited about going to Chico. Maybe I would be able to see a friend or two while we spread our resumes. As we hit the outskirts of Chico, I was shocked. It had been ten years since I had been there. In those ten years there had been an explosion of growth. Where there had been grazing livestock and beautiful orchards, there was now a mall, and big-box stores, retail outlets, and industrial parks. Where had the charming little town, with a university, that I loved so much, gone? I was stunned. We found a hotel in the old part of Chico. That part of town brought back a slew of memories. Upon checking in, I headed to the city library to find addresses for social services agencies that we could visit the following day. Carolyn spent time playing with Jonathan and resting. I found a number of non-profit agencies that offered various services that we might be able to provide. I was really surprised that only four psychiatrists were listed in the Yellow Pages.

The next day, we started early and met some people and left resumes at the agencies I had found. We felt that it had been a successful morning. Later, Carolyn decided to call the county mental health department. From the time the county answered the phone, the Holy Spirit displayed His influence in everyday life. After a few minutes' conversation, Carolyn was invited to meet a couple of administrators at their office. I dropped her off and drove around Chico with Jonathan. About an hour later I stopped at a pay phone (we're still years away from cell phones) and called the office. I was told that Carolyn was on a tour of the hospital and other facilities with one of the administrators, and to call back in an hour. When I called back, Carolyn told me they wanted to interview me also. While they were touring, they mentioned that the county also hired social workers and marriage and family counselors. I didn't know what to think. I always saw myself having a private practice. It never occurred to me there was another facet of the mental-health field I could qualify for. By mid-afternoon, we were back at the hotel trying to take in all that had happened. We quickly packed and checked out of the hotel. We needed to stick to our itinerary and drive to our next location, which was Auburn, a quaint community above Sacramento. We were elated about the events of the day. Carolyn left with everything but a signed contract from the county. I'm not sure, but I think we were floating about an inch off the road as we drove.

Upon our checking into a hotel in Auburn, we anticipated a wonderful Sabbath. We had much to praise God for. After dinner, Jonathan started being fussy. He quickly escalated to angry cries, which got worse as the evening progressed. I was thankful Carolyn had chosen a one-year pediatric internship after her brief hiatus following medical school. She used that experience to evaluate him. He had quickly developed a high temperature. I started praying, asking for wisdom. Carolyn decided to immerse him in a tepid bath. This brought the temperature down a bit, but Jonathan was very uncomfortable. He slept little that night. Sabbath morning, I decided to go to the local church for prayer and worship. Jonathan was sleeping when I left. This was his first illness, and the emotional impact on me was new and weighty. When I returned, Carolyn had Jonathan back in the bath. After praying once again, we decided to head back home. We briefly drove around town, then headed down the freeway. We didn't leave any resumes or make any stops. We decided to bypass the last two stops on our itinerary and return home as soon as possible. We got as far as Fresno, in the central valley, when we decided Jonathan wasn't getting better. We pulled into Fresno Memorial Hospital Emergency Room. Upon an examination, Jonathan was given a small dose of antibiotic and we were on our way. Before leaving Auburn, we purchased a foam cooler and some ice. So Carolyn was able to give Jonathan a cool compress when needed. When we returned to Glendale, he seemed a little better. When he woke up the next morning, he was back to his rascally self. Praise God!

We spent that evening reviewing out trip. Though it didn't turn out as planned, all that happened in Butte County was exciting. And it proved that Carolyn was a prophetess when she said it would be a wasted trip if we didn't go to Chico. At least in that situation she was!

The next day, I went to the Glendale library. I wanted to look for some more information about county mental health systems. I learned that each county, by law, was supposed to provide a system. To my surprise, one whole rack in the library was filled with telephone books from every county in the state. With the help of a map, I identified seventeen counties in Northern and Central California that I thought might be good places to live. Though events in Butte County were promising, I wanted to give Jesus latitude in finding our new home. So I started using the seeking-and-finding principle of Matthew 7:7–8. What a God of wisdom, providing all the promises of Scripture to help us as we sojourn through this world.

Each county had an phone number to call for information regarding employment. I called all seventeen counties and listened to their recordings of job opportunities. It turned out that every county had openings in their mental-health departments. Some for me and some for Carolyn. But not one, *not one*, had an opportunity for both of us! At least we both had had interviews with Butte County. The final outcome of our trip north remained to be seen.

14.

Trial and Faithfulness, God's Faithfulness

Two days later, I received a call from a couple of non-profit agencies in Butte County about the resumes we had dropped off. They conducted phone interviews and asked me to let them know when I was coming to Chico again. I was excited about the response from our "leaves of autumn" endeavor. I wondered how many replies we would have received if we had been able to follow our full itinerary. We rejoiced in all that was happening. We were amazed, once again, at how God can arrange situations to blend together in order to reveal His plans. The next day, I received a call from one of the supervisors from Butte County Mental Health. She was the director of the in-patient hospital in Chico. She informed me that she didn't have any regular-help positions (full-time with benefits) at that time, but she had an extra-help budget (hourly pay) available. She offered full-time work on that basis. All of a sudden, I had three opportunities to choose from.

Everything was progressing tremendously. It was thrilling. For me, I get enthused and grateful when I suspect that Jesus is manifesting His will in our lives and revealing His plans to us. For the next few weeks, we continued with work and my internships. It continued to be a slow struggle to accumulate my hours. I was about halfway to my goal of 3,000, but it was frustrating. Carolyn continued to enjoy her work even as she started to bulge. Jonathan, our young son, always seemed to have a good time.

> *We were amazed, once again, at how God can arrange situations to blend together in order to reveal His plans.*

I decided to contact our realtor and see whether home values were returning to the levels they were at before the economy fell. She reported that the market was struggling to regain value. Condominium sales, in particular, were lagging. That news was a little disconcerting to me. What if we couldn't sell the condo if God opened the way for us to move? Then I remembered that the situation was in God's hands. I figured that if we were going to move, Jesus would sell the condo in His time. I apprised the realtor of our developing plan and asked her to keep us in mind.

In the midst of all the happenings, I received a call from my sister. It looked as if she would soon have to place my mother in a residential facility. As with all the other treatments my mother had endured, the positive effects of the gold shots were diminishing. My heart was heavy. She had suffered so much pain and loss of freedom because of her arthritis. How much can one tolerate? I called her and she was in good spirits. She had always been a trooper. I yearn for Jesus to come and end all the pain and suffering of this world.

Carolyn was expanding quite a bit when we decided it was time to return to Chico. She'd had a couple of brief contacts with the administrator at the Butte County Mental Health Department since we returned from our first trip. It seemed assured that she would have a position if we moved to Chico. She was willing to take a part-time position once our daughter was born. Yes, a girl! I alerted the non-profit agencies who had interviewed me that I was coming. It was late winter, and we were praying for decent weather for the drive. We were hopeful that the blessings from our last trip would be consummated as we met with potential employers. Since my outcome remained up in the air, I was spending more time in prayer than usual. This was a big deal, not just for my family, but for me. If everything worked out for us, I would be returning to my beloved Chico after being away for about ten years. What an amazing God! I would complete a full circle. I was surely different from the person I was when I left. I had begun a healing journey, given a new family, more education, and a new career. One early morning, as these possible events were whirling through my head, I was humbled by what Jesus had engineered in my life. He truly was the engineer, I was back in the caboose, at times, holding on for dear life.

We were blessed with fair weather on the trip north. We took more days off this time because we didn't know what was going to happen when we arrived. We were tingling, even giddy, with anticipation. We drove all day and checked into a hotel and relaxed that evening. The next day I called the two non-profit agencies to set up interviews. Then I called the mental health department. I told them I couldn't make the first appointment they offered because I had another interview scheduled. The following day I had the two interviews with the non-profit agencies. They both had group homes for emotionally disturbed children and offered family therapy. I thought the interviews went well. At about the same time, Carolyn was signing a contract with the county.

The following day, I met with the supervisor from the mental health department. I was officially offered a full-time extra-help position on the in-patient unit. Legally it was called the psychiatric health facility (PHF, affectionately known as the Puff). This mini hospital had twenty-two beds; it was where county agencies like law enforcement, schools, social services, and the community at large would bring people who were out of control in public (not alcohol or substance related), mental-health patients who had stopped taking their medication, suicidal individuals, and people with various other issues. Wow! This was quite different from anything I had been involved with in my internships. Was this what I wanted to do? As far as gaining experience, it would be like starting all over again. I told the supervisor I would think it over that night and call her the following day. That night I prayerfully looked over all the paperwork and brochures I had been given by the three agencies. Early the next morning, I received a call from one of the head administrators Carolyn had been talking with. Upon finding out that I hadn't made a decision yet, she asked me to meet someone who worked on the PHF unit. Someone who did the same work that I would be doing. Lord Jesus, please make things clear about which position to take.

So that afternoon I met with Mac, the gentleman from the PHF unit. We hit it off immediately. He was both humorous and informative. A former police officer who had transitioned to being a marriage and family counselor, he was also a Christian. He gave me an overview of the function of the PHF and what I would be doing; that, along with a guided tour. When we returned to his office, he asked which non-profit agencies I had interviewed with. I didn't know it until later, but he had been assigned the task of convincing me to pick the PHF position. He gave me a blank piece of paper, had me put a line down the middle to make two columns, then asked me a series of questions about the information I had received from the agencies. After a while, it became obvious that the PHF position and Butte County's pay scale and benefits were superior to those of the non-profit agencies. All the notations I had made were in the same column. He told me that I could accumulate my intern hours more quickly working on the PHF. That sealed the deal! I had asked Jesus to make it clear which agency He wanted me to work at. He answered my prayer with clarity. All these years later, Mac and I remain close friends.

I contacted the non-profits to thank them for their consideration and inform them of my decision. We stayed one more day and then headed home. Although indications were positive after our first trip to Chico, there remained unknowns. Those unknowns had now been swept away by the working of the Holy Spirit. Also, matters at home would be taken care of. When God moves in a situation, He takes care of the whole ball of wax, from first to last, from beginning to end. So I wouldn't have to worry about the myriad issues that come up in making a long-distance move, such as what to do with the condo.

But I did worry about the condo. I definitely wanted to sell. I didn't feel comfortable being 600 miles away from our one-and-only major investment. So when we returned, we contacted our realtor to inform her of what had happened on the trip and asked her to put the condo back on the market. She knew there was a time constraint and scheduled a couple of open houses. We went as low as we could on the asking price. I was pleading with the Lord about the sale.

In late spring, a little package from heaven arrived, and Rachel rounded out our family. Everything went well for Mom and baby. She was born on May 25, 1993. My joy knew no bounds as I held my daughter for the first time. She was so cute! What a Creator I have who can, by his word, bring into being such beauty. "For He spoke, and it was *done*; He commanded, and it stood fast" (Ps. 33:9).

After about three months the condo hadn't sold. In fact, there wasn't a single bid on it—not even a low-ball offer. I talked about the situation with Jesus, pleading with Him for a sale, right up to when the moving van left. Reluctantly, I found a property management firm to take over the condo. For the next three years or so, I had a running debate with Jesus about the sale of the condo. Finally, I decided to drop my argument. Jesus must have a plan, right? Actually, everything went well with the condo during the eight-plus years we leased it. The property managers found a great tenant, a musician with Disney who traveled the world doing projects. He was gone almost all the time and kept the place immaculate. Not one appliance needed replacing. There were no repair bills of any kind for those eight years. The only cost involved was a $35-per-month fee to the property managers! That's not a typo. Just $35 a month. The lease covered our mortgage and then some, each month. Obviously, Jesus knew what He was doing. *Oh, me of little faith.*

The rest of this condo story was quite humbling for me and glorifying for Jesus. It had been about eight years since we'd moved. All of a sudden, we began receiving post cards from realtors asking if we wanted to sell our condo. I'd say we received eight or ten over a couple of weeks. We wondered what was happening, so we called the realtor who had helped us previously. She said the market had been gradually coming back but lately had exploded. We asked her to put it back on the market. She called back a few days later with the news that someone wanted to buy the condo for cash. The interesting part is that the purchaser had never even seen the condo. We made the sale and, not surprising, the price was more than amenable. God's timing was perfect, and the realtor earned a nice commission.

A couple of months earlier, we had been discussing what we were going to do about our vehicle situation. My ancient Volvo was a blessed machine, but it was worn out. Also, the kids were getting to the age when they needed more room and, in the coming years, there would be teen-agers to cart around. We wanted a van but didn't have the funds to buy one. Except for the mortgage, we had a strategy of not going into debt to make a purchase. We had savings, but it wasn't nearly enough for a van. So when the proceeds from the sale of the condo came, we had enough after tithe, to purchase a new 2001 Honda Odyssey. I still shake my head when I think how much time and energy I spent debating with Jesus about not selling the condo. And exhibiting my lack of faith! Once again, the God who sees the future and knows our needs before we do, blessed a thick-headed sinner like me.

In preparation for the move, I took a solo trip to Chico to find a place to live. On the trip up, I stopped in to see my mother and her new living situation. My sister had done well. Carolyn and I decided to rent for a couple of months while we settled in to work and new surroundings. We wanted to buy a home, but we didn't know much about the real-estate market. I found a nice, small two-bedroom apartment with some open space outside the front door. I picked up some real-estate magazines on the way out of town. When I returned home, we were almost ready to go. Rachel was only about a month old. We wanted to move so we could settle in before starting work. One good thing about living in a small condo is that you don't have a lot of stuff. A small moving van carried all our goods to Chico.

Once settled, I had an amazing time. Just about everywhere we went in town, I ran into people I hadn't seen in years. It got to the point where we would guess whether we were going to see someone I knew. Showing up at the Chico church where I first attended was an emotional feast. Someone who had been a babe in Christ years earlier welcomed me warmly. Carolyn had an answer to prayer when she found a lady in Sabbath School who took little ones into the "school" at her home. I called a couple of friends for recommendations. She was highly praised and turned out to be excellent. Leaving the kids was not easy, especially with Rachel being so young. It ended up being only a few hours a week, though, as Carolyn was working part time.

Even though we didn't have much, our apartment was full of furniture and boxes, filling every nook and cranny. It was okay because we figured we would be there a couple of months at most. We started looking at houses as often as we could. Two months turned to three, then four. The apartment seemed to be shrinking with each passing week. We couldn't find anything we liked in Chico. We decided to expand our search to the various little towns near Chico. We even tried little mountain communities that were within driving distance. Finally, we linked up with a real-estate agent to help us. After a couple more months went by, I began wondering what the Lord had in store for us and why it was taking so long. The walls in our apartment were slowly closing in on us. We hadn't settled on a church yet, either. Finally, in exasperation, we told God we would go to the church nearest to the house He would give us.

After a couple more months went by, Carolyn woke me up in the middle of the night to inform me that she had been up praying. God strongly made clear to her she would find the house the following day. I turned over and went back to sleep. She was off from work the next day, so she took the kids and went up the hill to a little town called Paradise. She went without our agent. Her plan was to follow *for sale* signs as soon as she hit town. She did so, and found two homes she liked from the outside. One was brand-new; the other was an older two-story home situated in a secluded area off one of the main streets in town. She came home excited and contacted our agent to set up a tour in Paradise including the two houses she had found. That weekend the agent took us to see five homes. Of the five, the two Carolyn found were possibilities. After seeing the inside of the new house, she fell in love with the modern kitchen and vaulted ceilings. The house was so new, a fence hadn't been built yet. Then we took a look at the older house. When we walked in, I felt cramped. The ceilings were substandard, and it was over furnished. After the new house and high ceilings, this one felt like a cave. We didn't stay long.

We decided to put in a bid for the new house. Our realtor told us that a young couple had already made a bid for the property. We weren't sure what to do, but we wanted to, at least, be considered for the house. We bid $10,000 over the asking price. We felt that if this was the house God wanted us to have, we would have it. The contractor who built the house was also the owner. He called us the next day and told us he was selling the house to the couple. Even though we bid more, he felt obligated to sell the house to them. Carolyn was very disappointed. I wondered if we would ever get out of the hole-in-the-wall apartment. The following day we asked the agent to schedule a time for us to again see the other house Carolyn had found. It was inadequate throughout, with a truly one-person kitchen. The only allure from our first visit was that it had four bedrooms. It wasn't very appealing until we stepped out on the back deck. The yard needed a lot of work but there were fruit and nut trees, a beautiful barn with a corral, and a large pasture that stretched out behind the barn. I thought immediately of Rachel and a horse. We hadn't seen any of this the first time we visited. The property was 1.7 acres with a stream on the back boundary with wild berries everywhere. The overall property made the house seem not so bad. It had a rural feel to it. I told Carolyn if we bought the house, remodeling would be a priority.

The agent told us that the property had been up for sale for more than a year and had been reduced a few times. We decided that since Carolyn felt the Lord had impressed upon her that she would find the house, this must be it. So without the agent's knowledge, we prayerfully decided on the amount we would pay for the property. When she negotiated with the owners, they came up with a final asking price that came within $300 of our maximum. Praise God! We were as sure as sure can be that Jesus had saved the house for more than a year just for us. After a year we took out a second mortgage and remodeled and expanded by turning the three-car garage into a family room, laundry, and office for me. The house truly turned out to be a blessing for our family. We were there for the next twenty-five years. But it didn't end there. Jesus was watching out for us again. The church and academy were within a mile of our new home. We were set up for the next twelve years of Christian education for our kids.

After a year working on the PHF unit, I was offered a regular-help position with youth services, working with emotionally disturbed kids and their families. Securing health insurance and retirement turned out to be a real blessing. God certainly knew what He was doing in our lives. Leaving the PHF was difficult because of friendships, especially Mac, and the experience I gained. Mac and I had a lot of fun during that year. Mental-health work can be very grim. If you don't have some humor to break the stress, you can be devastated by the anguish of helping people and their families deal with a lifelong disruption.

One incident was particularly difficult. The first client I was assigned was a seventy-three-year-old man who was placed on the unit due to suicidal ideation. He had recently lost his wife to an illness. I had to catch on quickly to my responsibilities. Every breath was a prayer. After working up a comprehensive history, stabilizing him with other staff, and consulting with family and the psychiatrist, I set up an extensive after-care plan for him. Things like his going to a nearby doughnut shop for socialization, giving his medication to his next-door neighbor for safety, and scheduled contact with his children. I had thirty-six items all together. When we decided he was stable, he was discharged to home. Every client deserves their freedom as soon as they are deemed safe. Sometimes it is a very difficult decision. Within a week he had committed suicide. I was stunned. What an introduction to the mental-health field! Prayer and my supervisor helped me work through the issues.

Mac was right when he told me I would accumulate my intern hours quickly on the PHF. The hours were certified by the state and I was eligible to take the written exam. This was an obstacle for me because of my poor study and test-taking skills. The old fear and anxiety emerged. I did a lot of praying and studying for the hundred-question exam. When I received my exam date, a notice was attached indicating that for the first time, a new computer-generated test was going to be used. This information didn't alleviate any of my anxiety. I wasn't totally illiterate on the computer, but I certainly wasn't Steve Jobs. The description of the exam seemed straightforward enough. The night before, I spent time with Jesus, asking for peace more than anything. When I walked into the exam site, I was surprised that I was the first one there. There must have been seventy-five computers set up. When the time for the exam came, a man came in and registered me and said I could begin. I could not believe it! *I was the only one taking the test.* That vast room filled with computers— empty. Talk about answering my prayer for peace! Usually there would be an atmosphere thick with stress and anxiety from a room filled with interns with years of effort on the line. Without anybody there, I was able to relax and put my feet up. After the exam, there was an almost immediate readout of my results. It didn't give a score, just a *pass* or *fail*. I PASSED! I never found out why I was the only one there.

I now had six months to prepare for the final step, the oral exam. The exam was controversial because it had a high failure rate. Somewhere in the decades that followed, it was dropped. But it was a reality for me. A failure meant waiting another six months. Mac had helped a few people prepare for the orals, so I worked with him. When the time came for the exam, I drove the eighty miles to Sacramento, where the test was held in a large hotel. An entire floor was reserved for the testing. Two examiners would give each intern a sample case to evaluate and answer a series of questions about how they would handle it. Since my room was in another area of the hotel and my exam time wasn't until 1:30 pm, I sat in the lobby most of the morning, watching people coming and going. The stress was palpable. You could tell who was an intern and who wasn't. I decided to check out the floor where the exam was held, and struck up a conversation with one of the registrars. She asked when my appointment was, and when I told her 1:30, she said I should go early; since some examiners came back from lunch early, I might not have to wait as long.

I went downstairs again. Suddenly I started feeling as if I were coming down with the flu. I went back to my room instead of eating lunch. I flopped on the bed and began praying, pleading with God that I wasn't coming down with the flu. After a while, I rolled off the bed and onto my knees, with my Bible on the bed. I wasn't feeling any worse, but not any better, either. I was praying for strength to make it through the exam. I opened my Bible, and the Holy Spirit went to work. I opened to Exodus 4:12, which was a promise I had never seen before. Moses is complaining to the Lord for calling him to deliver Israel. Moses declares that he isn't eloquent in speech. God's reply to Moses blew my mind. "Now therefore, go, and I will be with your mouth and teach you what you shall say." Wow, what a timely promise! It is hard to put into words how I reacted. Overwhelmed, grateful, flabbergasted, relieved, astonished. I don't really remember. How the Spirit does these things is beyond me! Why am I the beneficiary of such blessings? It could only be God's mercy as He looked down on a helpless sinner in great need.

I took the advice of the registrar and arrived early. I checked in and went to the notorious high-stress waiting room. I was the only one there! Within five minutes, somebody called my name, and I went in for the exam. The registrar's advice had been a Godsend. I did what I could with the case as it was presented.

I immediately drove the eighty miles home. I was groggy all the way but greatly relieved. Now I just had to wait for my results to arrive in the mail. If God gives you a promise like He did to me, you have to believe He would fulfill. Amazing, He would teach me "what you will say." Praise

His holy name! Nevertheless, I had to wait several weeks. The day after Thanksgiving 1994, a large envelope arrived in the mail from the licensing board. As any intern knew, a large envelope was good; a regular-sized one was bad. Finally, after almost nine years Jesus, nudged me across the finish line. A reluctant student deceived by the big lie, constantly battling fear and anxiety—by God's grace, I made it.

For the next several years, Carolyn and I continued working for the county, and the kids continued to grow. I didn't know it, but a hurricane was headed my way at work. I'm usually regarded as an easygoing, laid-back, sixties type of guy. But at work I was a real "type A." I also had a streak of perfectionism. I want things to work out right, to be done correctly. Perfectionism is a challenging way to encounter an imperfect world with imperfect people. As I passed the age of fifty, work started getting tough. Every assignment seemed to go wrong. I was moved from program to program. In my stubbornness, I was unable to perceive what was happening. I just continued to push forward as I always had. Looking back, I see that Jesus was giving me some warning signs. But I didn't heed them.

After a couple of years of increasing difficulty, I became depressed and found myself taking anti-depressants. *The counselor started seeing a counselor.* Not uncommon. In therapy I was helped to see that I was not only depressed, but also experiencing mid-life issues. A short definition of burnout is pushing your emotional gas pedal to the floor and getting no response. I was drained. The upshot of this trauma was that I was forced to retire in 2003, at the age of fifty-five, or face a possible breakdown. Where was Jesus during this chaos? He was right where He always is, right by my side. "For I, the LORD your God, will hold your right hand, saying to you, 'Fear not, I will help you'" (Isa. 41:13). I learned a great deal about myself through the raging waters of this experience, which I made more difficult because of my stubbornness. My bullheaded approach to my work life was the cause of many of my problems. It took me about five years to recover fully from the burnout. Today I have much more peace in my life. Jesus changed me through this ordeal.

I found out just how much Jesus changed me when, about three years after retiring, I went back to work with the county as extra help. Mac had become a supervisor at the Paradise Center and asked me to help him with a new program he was heading up. I noticed immediately that I was different. The bull in the China shop had mellowed dramatically. The program lasted a year, then closed down. After another year or so I began the most enjoyable phase of my counseling career when I joined, as a volunteer, the chaplain's department at Feather River Adventist Hospital in Paradise. They used me in various ways beside just visiting patients'

> *I am convinced that forgiveness is the greatest healing power God has given us. Forgiveness is the center of the Gospel!*

bedsides. I would wander through the hospital and pray with family members who were anxiously waiting for word about a loved one. The waiting room of the intensive care unit was particularly interesting to me because of the heavy burdens carried by the people there.

Then I was asked to join a team with a doctor and the chaplain. The doctor was a chronic-pain specialist who had developed a program that would help his chronic-pain patients beyond the use of addictive pain medications. Part of the program involved a large group meeting of the patients. We met once every two weeks for lectures on various topics with about twenty-five to forty patients. I would end up working with an occasional client from that group. God really blessed those meetings. One of my presentations was on forgiveness. We saw some miracles in that group. I am convinced that forgiveness is the greatest healing power God has given us. Forgiveness is the center of the Gospel!

In addition to working at the hospital, I would see people in my home office, free of charge. I'd had a small private practice in that office for years. Now I enjoyed pure ministry by not charging a fee. Most would have not been able to pay, anyway. This was a fulfilling time for me. Between the hospital and my home office, I would have anywhere from eleven to eighteen hours of ministry a week. It was just about right.

During those years, both kids graduated from Paradise Adventist Academy and went off to college. Jonathan is working as a certified public account and Rachel is a registered nurse. We were truly blessed when Jesus reserved that home for us and led Carolyn to it at the perfect time. Praise God!

As time went by and the kids were grown, Carolyn started working full time. After a few years, she was named medical director for what is now called the Butte County Department of Behavioral Health. Her duties consisted of supervising a staff of psychiatrists, testifying in court, participating on committees, and serving as the doctor for the PHF. A burnout job if ever there was one! She liked the position and, along with a new department director, the agency had several years of smooth sailing. But her husband, who understood burnout, was very concerned and watchful as the years went by. In 2018, her fifth year as medical director, she came home one night and simply stated, "I need to retire."

She had finally hit burnout; the stress had overcome her. But she wasn't as stubborn as I was. She didn't keep butting her head against the wall like I did, so her burnout was less imposing. Praise God. Still, she was in pretty bad shape, especially after letting down her façade and announcing that she was retiring. In the county system, a retirement is usually planned many months ahead, maybe even a year. It takes an individual, the county, and the state a great deal of time to coordinate all the decisions and paperwork involved in a retirement.

But Jesus came to the rescue. The process that usually took several months was completed in just one month. When we went to the county administrative offices, Carolyn wondered whether filling out the plethora of paperwork was possible. I wondered if they would let me fill them out for her. When we sat down with the benefits representative, she told us she had taken the liberty of filling out the papers for Carolyn. Thank you, Jesus! All Carolyn had to do was sign her name a few times. Later on, Carolyn thought that maybe her boss had directed the lady to make it as easy as possible and to fast-track the process. I was thankful. Carolyn's retirement led to many changes in my health insurance and my retirement and social-security benefits. The Holy Spirit used the representative lady several times in the process. She seemed to anticipate any problem, answer every question we had, and caught any mistakes made by the state. She was an angel.

There are times during a marriage when a situation arises that causes massive change in the life of the couple. Marriage has stages and the challenges are different in each stage. We didn't know it at the time, but enormous change was about to take place, and it would test our faith and trust in God. All that was familiar, all that was comfortable, all that had meaning for us as a couple was to be challenged. It started with Carolyn's retirement and difficulty with burnout. She went to see her doctor in Chico for help. She reported that she had been having some minor female difficulties, which at her age was rare. She was scheduled at once for an ultrasound. When she received a call from the doctor with the results, she was immediately sent to a specialist for further testing. A biopsy showed that Carolyn had about a 40 percent risk of developing uterine cancer, and surgery was recommended. A life-changing moment for us. The surgery was successful. A couple of weeks later Carolyn received a final pathology report from Stanford Medical Center. She was stunned because the biopsy showed pockets of *full-blown cancer* in what had been removed. Stress is like fertilizer for cancer, and Carolyn certainly had her share of stress over the years. We were comforted in knowing that Jesus was with us every step of the way. He truly is the Great Physician. Carolyn's only follow-up is a yearly exam. So far, so good.

About a month or so later, Carolyn was informed by family members that her ninety-three-year-old mother had fallen and fractured her pelvis. Carolyn was the only one in the family who could tend to her; as the eldest child in her Japanese family, the responsibility fell on her shoulders. She would spend two weeks at a time in Ventura, California, where she had grown up. Her parents (father was also ninety-three years old) had lived in their home for over fifty years. She would come home for a couple days and then go back south. Our life together was changing.

On November 8, 2018, at seven o'clock, I was where I was almost every Thursday morning. In my office dialing the phone to connect with the Northern California Conference Prayer Line, a once-a-week prayer group. The blinds were drawn, so I had no idea what was happening outside. When the group was over, I left to get my car serviced. When I backed out of the garage, I noticed the sky was a strange color. When I got to the shop, the mechanic wasn't there. That was unusual, so I waited a few minutes. When he didn't show up, I left. The streets were busier than usual and the sky was darkening. Carolyn and I arrived home at about the same time. By then the sky was very dark and embers were starting to fall. We soon learned that our town was threatened by a fire in a nearby canyon. The wind was blowing harder than it ever had in all the years we'd been living in Paradise. We were part of a small group of residents that received an evacuation call. We sent up a prayer and hurriedly threw a few things in our cars. The Camp Fire was upon us. Much could be said about the most catastrophic wildfire in California's history.

It was fortunate for us that we escaped early and avoided some of the horrific, traumatic events some of our friends went through. We saw enough, though, believe me. It took us two and half hours to go six miles down to the valley. Exploding propane tanks made it sound like a war zone as we navigated the bumper-to-bumper throng. *We lost everything.* Our beautiful home of twenty-five years, everything we owned, our van that was still running strong. Everything but our cars. The fire was satanic. It burned super hot, even melting car bumpers. It was reported that the windblown fire was moving at one hundred yards per second. A football field a second. The California Department of Forestry and Fire Protection (Cal Fire) reported it took only about six hours for the whole town to burn. Estimates are that more than 10,000 homes were lost. Carolyn had planned to leave to go back to her parents, so when we made it to the valley, we hugged, thanked God for our protection, prayed for Paradise, and went our separate ways. I was stunned.

I don't remember how I got to a friend's house in Chico, but they put me up, off and on, for the next three months as I dealt with the aftermath of the disaster. Life was never the same again. Where was God during all of this? He was in the middle of the storm. The stories of miracles run into the thousands, about the God of heaven delivering people, sheltering people who were stranded, and so much more. He was there. "When you pass through the waters, I *will* be with you . . . When you walk through the fire, you shall not be burned, nor shall the flame scorch you. For I *am* the LORD your God" (Isa. 43:2–3).

The fire was so huge it threatened Chico, about twelve miles away; it was halted only by the freeway. The whole area was shrouded in smoke and darkness for weeks. It was surreal. Smoke was blown hundreds of miles away to the San Francisco Bay Area and beyond. People were walking around like zombies. It was the first time that masks were needed by the local population. I began dealing with my insurance company and the myriad problems the catastrophe presented. It ended up taking two months to sort everything out, meet with the insurance appraisers, and submit the claim.

While all that was going on, I was praying about what Carolyn and I were supposed to do for housing. Thousands of people descended on Chico and the surrounding area. There wasn't any housing, of any type, for miles. Chico was unable to handle the huge influx. Tent cities sprung up wherever there was asphalt. Shelters were overrun. Some of my friends made hasty house purchases or rented the few apartments available. It was a crisis. Carolyn and I were communicating daily about what we should do. As I was working with the insurance company, it became clearer and clearer that we should stay in Ventura for the foreseeable future. Her parents needed help in order to remain independent and we needed a place to stay. Upon making that decision, every avenue in Chico closed for us. I was hesitant, but as Jesus made His will clear, I surrendered and started for Ventura and a new life.

That new life almost didn't happen, except it appears that God had once again been looking to the future. In December of 2017, less than a year before the Camp Fire, the huge Thomas Fire destroyed 535 homes in the Ventura hills, where Carolyn's parents live. The fire ran for many miles, eventually threatening Santa Barbara thirty miles away. Her parents were visiting relatives out of town. Amazingly, their home survived the fire with very minimal outside damage. The houses on both sides of their home burned to the ground, along with several others on their street. A while after we moved there, it hit me: If her parents' house had burned down, they would have been living with us in Paradise when the Camp fire happened. We would have been looking for housing for two ninety-three-year-old parents—and ourselves. We would have been scrambling along with thousands of others looking for shelter. It is impossible to know the exact reason the parents' home survived. Only God knows that. But several needs were filled because of it.

Once again, the God of heaven had everything in control. I have shared earlier instances of the Lord's meeting our needs. Incredibly, He had provisions for needs I didn't know I had. After settling in, buying clothes, and trying to adjust to my new surroundings, the trauma of the fire was weighing heavily on me. I had been so busy since the fire, having free time gave me opportunity to talk with Jesus at length about my emotional state. It wasn't the best. I felt lost. That was the main issue. So I gave myself permission to live day by day. No agenda, no major responsibilities, just live one day at a time. I thought I was coming to Ventura mainly to help Carolyn's parents. Jesus had other reasons for me being there, also.

In Paradise there were doctors I had been seeing for years. The fire had disrupted all services, including medical. I needed to get established with new doctors in Ventura. I needed a dermatologist because of difficulties with basal cell cancer, which led to, over the years, several minor surgeries on my face. I also needed a urologist for my prostate problems. After a couple of months, I started having severe difficulties with my prostate, which led to major surgery. I was very thankful there was no cancer. It turned out to be a bigger surgery than I expected, however. I was completely out of it for five days in the hospital, needing twenty-four-hour care. The dermatologist I had seen a few days before the surgery found that a biopsy was needed on my forearm. During those five days in the hospital, the dermatologist was urgently trying to contact me, but my phone was turned off. The last day in the hospital, they were able to contact Carolyn. They asked her to have me call immediately. When I called, I could tell by the doctor's voice, something was up.

The biopsy on my arm revealed melanoma, a skin cancer. The doctor had already referred me to a surgeon to see if the cancer had spread. I was supposed to do as little movement as possible after the prostate surgery, but I found myself back at the hospital, this time for testing. Unfortunately, the testing revealed that the cancer had spread up my arm to a lymph node in my armpit. A couple of days later, I had more surgery, in same-day services, to cut out the cancer and the affected lymph node. At least I didn't have to stay in the hospital. Then I was referred to an oncologist for evaluation and treatment.

The recommendation was a year-long course of treatment with immunotherapy, July 2019 to June 2020. The treatment brought on overwhelming fatigue and other side effects. My bed was like a magnet for a year. When the treatment ended, I was told by the doctor that, by all indications, I was in remission. Praise God! The fatigue dissipated quickly; some of the side effects remain. Once again, I am overwhelmed

> *The Lord continually amazes me with the mercy, grace, and love poured out to me. Who am I to receive such kindness, such care, such blessing?*

by the mercy and love of God. Here I am, new in the area, needing services I didn't know I needed. The God of wisdom knew every doctor in Ventura and how to get me to the ones I needed, just when I needed them. The doctors He chose were top of the line. I was impressed by their expertise and reputation.

I am humbled by God's mercy and grace toward me. I have difficulty expressing in words the emotions that reside in my heart. The Lord continually amazes me with the mercy, grace, and love poured out to me. Who am I to receive such kindness, such care, such blessing? I'm no one special. It must be my deficiency that touches His heart. I have found that one of the greatest blessings in my life is knowing how much I need Jesus. Reviewing and writing about forty-five years of God's working in my life has caused my faith to grow exponentially. What a blessing! What a God! There simply are not enough exclamation points!

A few months before I completed my treatment, a pestilence engulfed the planet. It has changed the world, probably forever. As we all know, a mysterious virus has captured the world's attention. Over the last year or so, we humans have been tested with regard to such issues as personal freedom, trusting authority, sheltering-in-place, and isolation. The pandemic has been a disaster for the world economy. Many believers are being challenged in their faith. Where is God in all this? Is He still on the throne?

I hope that the story of God's working in my life has strengthened your faith that God's sovereignty is as it always has been. He is in control of the whole universe. For every Christian who believes in the return of Jesus, current events should be piquing their interest in prophecies such as the one in Luke 21:26–28: "Men's hearts failing them from fear, and the expectation of those things which are coming on the earth, for the powers of the heavens will be shaken. Then they see the Son of Man coming in a cloud with power and great glory. Now when these things begin to happen, look up and lift up your heads, because your redemption draws near." Come, Lord Jesus!

Epilogue

Well, there you have it. A story of God's spectacular participation in one man's life, as he faced the trials and problems of living in this world, many of which were of his own making. Isn't God something? I hope your faith has been renewed, and that your joy has increased, with a clearer understanding of how much Jesus loves you and wants to be the architect of your life. He *does* have a plan for you, a very specific plan. A plan, right now, to give you hope, joy, and peace. Words don't do justice in describing what Jesus has done for me. And He wants to perform similar feats in your life. I hope that my life story, with all its wrong turns and blunders, has shown you that Jesus has a better plan for each one of us. "I know the plans I have for you" (Jer. 29:11, NIV).

Every person is unique and special in God's eyes. Do you know that there is not another person like you in all of God's universe? God loves to create, and His creative ability is unlimited. Through the eons of time, He has been creating galaxies, solar systems, planets, and people—no two alike. Your distinct creation by the God of the universe makes you *one of a kind*. This is from where your true self-worth is derived. You were created by God and redeemed by Jesus when He went to the cross for you. No one can take that from you. There was a poster I would share with clients; it showed a little girl saying, "God don't make no junk."

The foundation of my version of counseling is helping people see how an integral part of life is having a relationship with Jesus. It's known as *practical Christianity*. I believe Jesus wants to be involved in every aspect of our lives. I hope that seeing God's work in my life story has given you a deeper understanding of His desire to be involved in all that you do. All you have to do is invite Him into your daily life. It seems to me, one of the best ways to develop our faith is to test God by claiming His promises in the Bible. Using these promises in everyday life helps Him to be more real to us. They certainly are instrumental to me as I stumble through my journey. Our God is a nearby God, not a distant entity living in another dimension. Sending Jesus to die for the world is the greatest evidence of His love and concern for us. His watchcare is so deep and so broad that He even takes care of the birds; how much more so for those for whom His Son died. A simple daily prayer could be something like this: "Heavenly Father, please reveal Yourself to me today in a new and deeper way. I claim Your promise to … . In Jesus' name, amen." There are thousands of promises in Scripture that God stakes His reputation on. They are included in the Bible to help us in our daily walk.

The Bible has more to offer than just God's promises; the most important, the most dynamic result of studying the Word is coming into the presence of the Infinite. The One who has all power, all love. The only One who knows how to satisfy the cravings of the sinful heart. The Bible should be read slowly, with thought and contemplation. By "chewing on the Word," we are encountering God Himself through the Holy Spirit. The Word produces life, Jesus' life, within us. To physically live, we must eat. In the spiritual realm it is the same. We need to eat of the Bread of Life, which is Jesus, and He is nowhere better revealed than in His Word, the Bible. We should tremble whenever we handle the Scriptures. The Bible is the most vital, powerful, and essential entity in our world.

When we meet Jesus, we are adopted into His family. We are full heirs to the genuine riches of the universe. God is our Father, Jesus is our elder Brother. In a healthy family, there is open communication. God wants open, honest, heart-to-heart interaction with His children. This is why He has provided the incredible avenue of prayer. Prayer is a two-way exchange with the Creator of the universe, our heavenly Father. Communing with God in prayer can be comforting, unburdening, and life changing. It is "as essential to growth in grace, and even to spiritual life itself, as is temporal food to physical well-being" (White, *Messages to Young People*, p. 115). It is also the freeway to claiming His many promises. Prayer needs to be an integral part of our daily lives, as you read in my story. I am so thankful for serving a God who is always available to talk to and is interested in my day-to-day needs.

Recounting God's leading in my life has been most satisfying these past few months. Only the Holy Spirit could have brought to remembrance the sequence of events I have shared with you. I hope you have been as blessed in reading this book as I have been in writing it. God is greater than we can possibly fathom, and Jesus is true to His word. I am a living, breathing example of this truth.

Bibliography

Southwest Radio Church. Statement of Faith, 1933. https://1ref.us/1q9 (accessed October 19, 2021).

White, Ellen G. *Christ's Object Lessons*. Washington, DC: Review and Herald Publishing Association, 1900.

_____. *The Desire of Ages*. Mountain View, CA: Pacific Press Publishing Association, 1898.

_____. *Education*. Mountain View, CA: Pacific Press Publishing Association, 1903.

_____. *The Faith I Live By*. Washington, DC: Review and Herald Publishing Association, 1958.

_____. *In Heavenly Places*. Washington, DC: Review and Herald Publishing Association, 1967.

_____. *Manuscript Releases*. Vol. 9. Silver Spring, MD: Ellen G. White Estate, 1990.

_____. *Messages to Young People*. Hagerstown, MD: Review and Herald Publishing Association, 1930.

_____. *Prophets and Kings*. Mountain View, CA: Pacific Press Publishing Association, 1917.

_____. *Steps to Christ*. Mountain View, CA: Pacific Press Publishing Association, 1892.

_____. *Testimonies for the Church*. Vol. 1. Mountain View, CA: Pacific Press Publishing Association, 1868.

_____. *Thoughts from the Mount of Blessing*. Mountain View, CA: Pacific Press Publishing Association, 1896.

TEACH Services, Inc.
P U B L I S H I N G

We invite you to view the complete
selection of titles we publish at:
www.TEACHServices.com

We encourage you to write us
with your thoughts about this,
or any other book we publish at:
info@TEACHServices.com

TEACH Services' titles may be purchased in
bulk quantities for educational, fund-raising,
business, or promotional use.
bulksales@TEACHServices.com

Finally, if you are interested in seeing
your own book in print, please contact us at:
publishing@TEACHServices.com
We are happy to review your manuscript at no charge.

CPSIA information can be obtained
at www.ICGtesting.com
Printed in the USA
JSHW040111270522
26383JS00005B/166